D0127785

ICON

International Communication Through English

Donald Freeman

Kathleen Graves

Linda Lee

**McGraw-Hill
ESL/ELT**

ICON International Communication through English, 1st Edition

Published by McGraw-Hill ESL/ELT, a business unit of The McGraw-Hill Companies, Inc. 1221 Avenue of the Americas, New York, NY 10020. Copyright © 2005 by The McGraw-Hill Companies, Inc. All rights reserved. No part of this publication may be reproduced or distributed in any form or by any means, or stored in a database or retrieval system, without the prior written consent of The McGraw-Hill Companies, Inc., including, but not limited to, in any network or other electronic storage or transmission, or broadcast for distance learning.

1 2 3 4 5 6 7 8 9 10   KGP 09 08 07 06 05 04

ISBN: 0-07-255039-2

Editorial director: Tina B. Carver
Senior sponsoring editor: Thomas Healy
Senior development editor: Nancy Jordan
Production manager: Juanita Thompson
Interior designer: Nesbitt Graphics, Inc.
Cover designer: Nesbitt Graphics, Inc.
Illustrators: Reggie Holladay, Bill Petersen, Jonathan Massie
Photo research: Nesbitt Graphics, Inc.

ICON 1 Components

Student Book	0-07-255039-2
Workbook	0-07-255040-6
Teacher's Manual	0-07-255041-4
Audio Cassettes	0-07-255042-2
Audio CDs	0-07-255043-0

ICON Teaching-Learning Video   0-07-301662-4

Acknowledgments

The authors would like to thank the many people around the world who have provided invaluable feedback through reviewing and class testing ICON. In particular, we would like to thank:

Nely Barbosa Brock, Ana Carla Calabria, Roberto Soares Dias Junior, Julita Ribeiro Ferreira, Patricia Norma Gilardi, Itana de Almeida Lins, Juliana Valadares, **ACBEU,** Salvador, Brazil; Dr. Nicholas Dimmitt, **Asian Institute of Technology,** Thailand; Paul Humphries and Dee Parker, **AUA,** Bangkok, Thailand; Silvia Correa, Sonia Hobbs, Adriana Beneduzzi Passarelli, Jean Ewert Santos, Luiz Otavio de Barros Souza, Marilia de Moura Zanella, **Associação Alumni,** São Paulo, Brazil; Tsylla Balbino, Isabela Villas Boas, Marcella Ferreira Brotto, Carla Arena de Aquino, Maria da Luz Silva Delfino, Aldenir Brito de Sousa, Flavio Mariano, Rosangela Tiyoko Matsunaga, Ana Maria Pohl, Vania Rodgrigues, **Casa Thomas Jefferson,** Brasilia, Brazil; Yu-Chen Hsu, **Central University,** Taiwan; Shu-Fen Huang, **Chung Wen University,** Taiwan; Kathi Jordan, **Contra Costa College,** California; Shou-Shen Lu, **Cultural University,** Taiwan; Patrick Hwang, **E.Future,** Korea; Chi-Rei Ting, Li-Chi Yueh, **Fu Jen University,** Taiwan; Laura MacGregor, **Gakushkin University,** Tokyo, Japan; Greg Cossu, **Greg's English,** Takarazuka, Japan; Joe Luckett, Wilma Luth, **Hokusei Gakuen University,** Hokkaido, Japan; Michel Englebert, Rebecca Fletcher, Joo-Kyung Park, **Honam University,** Korea; Shi-Yun Huang, **Hsin Pu Technology Institute,** Taiwan; Sonia Bueno, Rosali Erlich, Monica Alcantara Marzullo, Doraliz Nogueira, Zaquia Lavi Tabach, **IBEU,** Rio de Janeiro, Brazil; David McMurray,

Kagoshima International University, Japan; Robin Strickler, **Kansai Gaidai University,** Osaka, Japan; Alexis Kim, Korea; Louie Dragut, Michelle Kim, Kevin Price, Neal D. Williams, **Kyung Hee University,** Seoul, Korea; Kazuyoshi Sato, **Nagoya University of Foreign Studies,** Japan; Johanna Katchen, **National Tsing Hua University,** Hsinchu, Taiwan; Aaron Campbell, Barbara Stein, **Ryukoku University,** Japan; Susana Christie, **San Diego State University,** California; Sally Gearhart, **Santa Rosa Community College,** California; Dr. Won Moon Song, **Silla University,** Pusan, Korea; Tai-Yung Lee, Yu-Hwa Lee, **Soo Chow University,** Taipei, Taiwan; Fairlie Atkinson, Damian Benstead, Kevin McEwen, Ron Schafrik, Nathan Stewart, **Sungkyunkwan University,** Seoul, Korea; Kathleen Tice, Richard Tice, **Soonchunhyang University,** Korea; Shi-Tei Shai, **Taipei Business Institute,** Taiwan; Co-Chon Tsai, Chung-Jei Tsen, **Taipei Technology Institute, Taiwan;** Ann-Marie Hadzima, **Taiwan National University,** Taipei; Lourdes Solis, **Technological Institute of Monterrey,** Mexico; Patricia Krejcik, Rosemarie A. Lemmerman, Aurea Camargo Ribeiro, Ligia Salgado Saad, **UCBEU, São Paulo,** Brazil; Dixie Santana, **Universidad Panamericana,** Guadalajara, Mexico; Morris Kimura, Hiromi Middleton, Tara O'Brien, **Vermont Adult Learning,** Vermont; Susan Dunlap, **West Contra Costa USD,** California.

We would also like to thank: Henry Hirschberg, Ed Stanford, Steve Van Thournout, Sam Costanzo, Tina Carver, Juanita Thompson, the exacting Nancy Jordan, and the inimitable Thomas Healy at McGraw-Hill. Thank you to Deborah Gordon for her creative work on the Infozones. Thanks also to Emily and Laura for their wise suggestions.

Contents

To the Teacher

ICON is a four-level integrated skills series that takes students from beginning to intermediate level. *ICON Book 1* is the high-beginning level of the series.

ICON grew out of an in-depth research project into the role of course books in effective teaching and learning. From this research the series has distilled a set of activity types that create effective learner interaction in the classroom. Each unit of *ICON Book 1* is designed around these core activities which were identified and developed through work with teachers who routinely teach at this language level. The core activities provide a structure which scaffolds the students' language-learning experience. The scaffolding is achieved in the following ways:

1. The activities are sequenced to build gradually and systematically from more tightly focused to more open-ended language-learning interactions.

2. The activity types recur throughout the book, making it easier for teachers to initiate student interaction in the class, since the activities become familiar to students.

3. Many activities are color-coded blue and yellow which clearly shows students *"who does what"*.

4. The units have a consistent structure which supports students' confidence and independence.

5. The target language is recycled within and across each unit of the book.

6. There are four review units (after Units 3, 6, 9 and 12) which help students review and consolidate what they have learned through pair work and information gap-activities.

This scaffolding makes *ICON* transparent and easy to use in both small and large classes.

COMPONENTS:

While the **Student Book** is the heart of the series, *ICON* has a concentric design; each component builds on and extends the others in an integrated, expanding system. The **Interleaved Teacher's Manual** gives detailed suggestions for how to use the Core Activities effectively, in addition to providing variations, expansion activities and culture notes. The **Teaching-Learning Video** (which is intended to be viewed by teachers and students) presents the Core Activities in short animated clips, clearly showing teachers and students alike how to participate in the *ICON* classroom. Through this integration of **Student Book**, **Teacher's Manual** and **Teaching-Learning Video**, the *ICON* series weaves together teaching and learning explicitly so that teachers and students can achieve their aims.

The following components are also available:

- The **Workbook** provides additional practice for students within or outside the classroom.

- The **Audio Program** (available as audio cassettes and audio CDs) contains recordings for all the listening activities in the Student Book. It features a variety of native English speakers in addition to some non-native voices and accents.

- The **Assessment Package** has placement, mid-course and final tests as well as comprehensive guidelines on how to assess oral communication.

ICON BOOK 1 CORE ACTIVITIES

YOU FIRST introduces students to target language which they can use immediately.

PRONUNCIATION is practiced in the context of the target language.

In **PAIR UP and TALK** and **REPORT**, students personalize learning by sharing their own preferences and experiences.

Activities are color-coded blue and yellow to make student interaction easier in large classes.

LISTENING activities introduce language in common situations. In addition, there are **GLOBAL INTERVIEWS** that present voices and opinions of people from around the world.

FOCUS ON IDIOMS highlights the English language as we really use it.

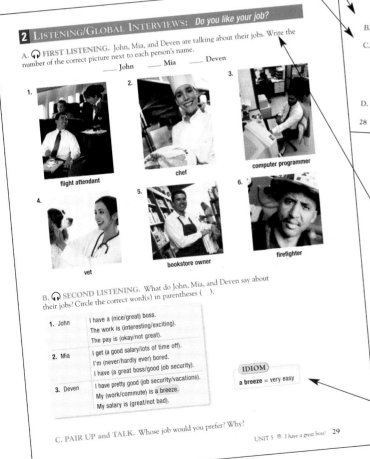

LANGUAGE FOCUS highlights language patterns and grammar points that serve communication.

MORE PRONUNCIATION PRACTICE provides additional pronunciation practice at the back of the book.

CONVERSATION STRATEGIES introduce students to simple but effective ways to manage and sustain conversations.

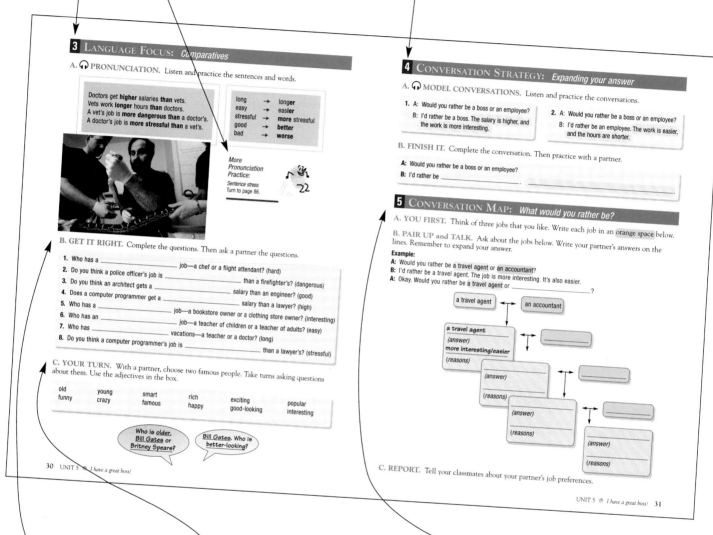

GET IT RIGHT focuses on language accuracy.

YOUR TURN encourages students to personalize the target language through games and communicative activities.

TALKATHONS, **ROLE PLAYS** and **CONVERSATION MAPS** get students to activate vocabulary, language patterns and conversation strategies in fun, communicative ways.

The **INFOZONE** presents information in an appealing magazine format, encouraging students to read, write and talk about the topic.

READ ABOUT IT, **TALK ABOUT IT** and **WRITE ABOUT IT** provide a step-by-step approach to reading and writing.

READ ABOUT IT helps students to understand the reading text and graphics.

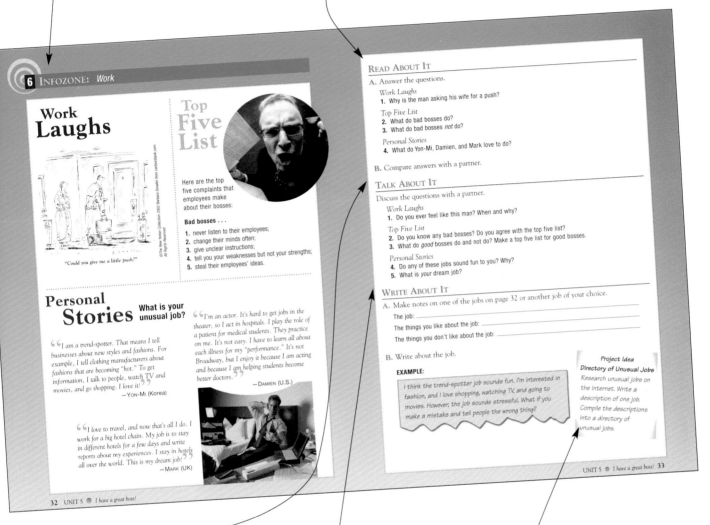

TALK ABOUT IT leads students to make inferences about the reading and to share opinions about the topic.

WRITE ABOUT IT has a pre-writing stage to help students develop their ideas.

PROJECT IDEA allows for expansion of the topic presented in the unit.

1 VOCABULARY: *Classroom habits*

A. YOU FIRST. Check (✓) your answers.

1. Do you ever come to class late?
- ☐ Yes, usually.
- ☐ Yes, sometimes.
- ☐ No, never.

2. Do you usually write down the homework assignment?
- ☐ Yes, usually.
- ☐ Yes, sometimes.
- ☐ No, never.

3. Do you ever doodle in class?
- ☐ Yes, usually.
- ☐ Yes, sometimes.
- ☐ No, never.

4. Do you usually look up new words?
- ☐ Yes, usually.
- ☐ Yes, sometimes.
- ☐ No, never.

5. Do you ever daydream in class?
- ☐ Yes, usually.
- ☐ Yes, sometimes.
- ☐ No, never.

6. Do you ever ask questions in class?
- ☐ Yes, usually.
- ☐ Yes, sometimes.
- ☐ No, never.

B. 🎧 PRONUNCIATION. Listen and practice the questions above.

C. PAIR UP and TALK. Ask a partner the questions.

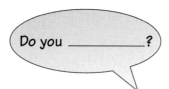

Do you _____?

Yes, sometimes.

D. REPORT. Tell your classmates one thing about your partner.

My partner _____.

A. LOOK/THINK/GUESS.

What's on the board? What kind of class is this?

What are the two people talking about?

B. 🎧 MODEL CONVERSATION. Listen and practice.

Meg: Zack!

Zack: Oh, hi, Meg. What's up?

Meg: Do you have today's homework assignment? I forgot to write it down.

Zack: Not again! You always forget!

Meg: Not always.

Zack: Well, almost always.

Meg: Okay, okay. What's the assignment?

Zack: Just a minute. Let me find it.

Meg: Thanks.

> **IDIOM**
>
> **What's up?** = What's new?

C. 🎧 ACTIVE LISTENING. Listen to the rest of the conversation. What does Zack tell Meg to do for homework? Circle a, b, or c.

1. Read the story on page _____ .	**a.** 23	**b.** 28	**c.** 63
2. _____ every new word.	**a.** Look up	**b.** Don't look up	
3. Answer the questions on page _____ .	**a.** 28	**b.** 29	**c.** 38
4. Write _____ .	**a.** one sentence	**b.** one paragraph	**c.** ten paragraphs

Did Zack give Meg the correct assignment?   ☐ Yes. ☐ No.

3 LANGUAGE FOCUS: *Frequency adverbs*

A. 🎧 **PRONUNCIATION.** Listen and practice.

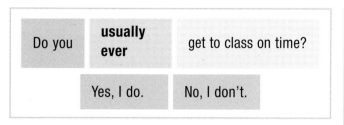

Do you	**usually** **ever**	get to class on time?
	Yes, I do.	No, I don't.

I	**always** **almost always** **usually** **sometimes** **hardly ever** **never**	get to class on time.

More
Pronunciation
Practice:

Intonation of "yes/no" questions
Turn to page 84.

B. GET IT RIGHT. Rewrite the questions and statements. Put the adverbs in the correct place. Then compare answers with a partner.

1. Do you do your homework in the morning? (usually)

Do you usually do your homework in the morning?

2. Do you forget to do your homework? (ever)

_____

3. Do you take notes in class? (usually)

_____

4. Do you speak your first language in class? (ever)

_____

5. I do my homework in the morning. (never)

_____

6. I forget to do my homework. (hardly ever)

_____

7. I take notes in class. (always)

_____

8. I speak my first language in class. (sometimes)

_____

C. YOUR TURN. Work with a partner. Take turns.

1. List five classroom habits. Four are **true** for you, but one is **not true**. You can use the ideas in the box or your own ideas.

2. Read the list to your partner. Your partner guesses which sentence is not true.

Example:

1. I usually get to class on time.
2. I sometimes fall asleep in class.

IDEAS

sit next to my friends

forget my books

chew gum

fall asleep

do homework in class

4 CONVERSATION STRATEGY: *Confirming what you heard*

A.  **PRONUNCIATION.** Listen and practice the questions.

Friday's class?

Did you say Friday's class?

Dot com?

Did you say dot com?

B. 🎧 **LISTEN and ADD.** Write the missing questions. Then practice with a partner.

1. A: Do you have the homework assignment from Friday's class?

B: _____

A: Yeah, I missed it. I was sick.

2. A: What's your e-mail address?

B: It's Marco at media dot net.

A: _____

B: No, dot net.

5 TALKATHON: *Language-learning strategies*

A. TALK AROUND. Interview two classmates. Write their answers in the chart. Ask follow-up questions. Remember to confirm what you heard.

Questions	_____'s answers	_____'s answers
1. Do you ever write e-mails in English?		
2. Did you watch a movie in English last month?		
3. How often do you listen to songs in English?		
4. Do you ever read English books or magazines?		
5. Did you use the Internet in English last week?		
6. How often do you speak English outside of class?		

B. REPORT. Tell something interesting you learned about a classmate.

In My Opinion

I teach English to teenagers and adults. Every year, some of my students tell me they aren't "good" language learners. Well, I believe that *everyone* can be a good language learner. Successful language learners use these important strategies:

- They aren't afraid to make mistakes. They learn from their mistakes!

- They often practice English outside of class.

- They use different ways to communicate. For example, when you don't know a word, you can use your hands to help you communicate.

"*Anyone who uses these simple strategies can be a "good" language learner!*"
— MARTHA (Canada)

Facts on File

In a recent survey, teachers reported five bad classroom habits that bother them the most. Teachers are most annoyed when students:

1. don't do the homework;
2. don't listen to the teacher or to the other students when they are talking;
3. talk to other students at the wrong time;
4. come to class late;
5. fall asleep in class.

Tips of the Day

What are your tips for learning new words?

"*When I see or hear a new word, I write it down in my little notebook. Later, I always write the new words on flashcards. Then I look up words in a dictionary and write the meanings on the back of the flashcards. My only problem is that I often forget to study the cards!*"
— WINNIE (Taiwan)

"*My first tip is to buy an English-English learner's dictionary. I prefer dictionaries with lots of pictures. The pictures help me to remember the words. My other tip is to try to use new words a few times the same day you learn them. That helps me a lot.*"
— EDGAR (Argentina)

READ ABOUT IT

A. Answer the questions.

In My Opinion
1. What does the teacher believe about "good" language learners?

Facts on File
2. Which "bad" study habit happens outside the classroom?

Tips of the Day
3. What problem does Winnie mention?
4. What kind of dictionary does Edgar like?

B. Compare answers with a partner.

TALK ABOUT IT

Discuss the questions with a partner.

In My Opinion
1. Do you agree that everyone can be a "good" language learner? Why or why not?
2. Which of the "good" language-learning strategies do you use?

Facts on File
3. Which "bad" study habits do you often see?
4. Which "bad" study habit do you think bothers your teacher the most?

Tips of the Day
5. Do you use any of these tips? If yes, which ones?
6. What do you do to learn new words?

WRITE ABOUT IT

A. Think of a good language-learning strategy that you use. Make notes.

What is the strategy? _____

Describe the strategy: _____

Tell how the strategy helps you: _____

B. Write about your language-learning strategy.

EXAMPLE:

I often watch videos of British or American movies. Usually I only watch 10 or 15 minutes each time. I don't understand everything, but I learn a lot of new words and idioms. Watching movies in English also helps my pronunciation.

Project Idea
Phrase Book for Tourists
Make a list of polite phrases and survival questions and answers for a visitor to your country. Include English translations.

I never watch soap operas.

1 VOCABULARY: *Kinds of TV shows*

A. YOU FIRST. *How often do you watch* _____ ? Write *almost every day, once a week, once in a while,* or *never* in the blanks.

1. sitcoms (situation comedies)

_____

2. sports

_____

3. talk shows

_____

4. game shows

_____

5. soap operas

_____

6. the news

_____

B. ∩ PRONUNCIATION. Listen and practice the questions above.

C. PAIR UP and TALK. Interview a partner about TV.

> How often do you watch sitcoms?

> Almost every day.

> What's your favorite sitcom?

> Why do you like sitcoms?

D. REPORT. What is one TV show you like but your partner doesn't like?

A. LOOK/THINK/GUESS. What kind of TV show is Zack watching? Why do you think so? What else is he doing?

B. 🎧 **MODEL CONVERSATION.** Listen and practice.

Zack:	Hello?
Ben:	Hi, Zack. What's happening?
Zack:	Not much. I'm just watching TV.
Ben:	Really? What's on?
Zack:	*The Bachelor.*
Ben:	Oh, yeah? What channel is it on?
Zack:	Channel 11.
Ben:	Channel 11? Okay, great.
Zack:	Ben? Are you there, Ben?
Ben:	Yeah, I'm here.
Zack:	So, why did you call?
Ben:	Sorry, Zack. I want to watch *The Bachelor.* Call me later, okay?

(IDIOM)

What's happening? =
What are you doing?

C. 🎧 **ACTIVE LISTENING.** Lucy, Pete, and Meg call Zack. What is each person's opinion of the show? Check (✓) *likes the show* or *doesn't like the show.*

Caller	likes the show	doesn't like the show
1. Lucy	☐	☐
2. Pete	☐	☐
3. Meg	☐	☐

A. 🎧 **PRONUNCIATION.** Listen and practice the questions.

What	's a good sitcom? channel is the news on? did you watch last night? kinds of TV shows do you like?	**Why**	are game shows popular? do you like soap operas? don't you like talk shows? didn't you watch the news last night?
When	is the news on? do you usually watch TV?	**How many**	TV shows do you watch regularly? hours of TV did you watch yesterday?

More Pronunciation Practice:

Intonation of "wh-" questions
Turn to page 84.

22

B. GET IT RIGHT. Unscramble the questions. Then compare with a partner.

1. hours a week / you / do / how many / watch TV

How many hours a week do you watch TV ?

2. favorite / your / what / TV / show / is

_____ ?

3. show / what kind / of / it / is

_____ ?

4. it / when / on / is

_____ ?

5. channel / on / what / is / it

_____ ?

6. do / it / like / you / why

_____ ?

7. shows / dislike / you / do / what kinds of

_____ ?

8. why / like / you / don't / them

_____ ?

C. YOUR TURN. Work with a partner. Take turns.

Student A: Think of a TV show you like to watch. Don't tell your partner!
Student B: Ask questions. Guess the TV show.

Example: B: What kind of show is it?

A: It's a game show.

B: When is it on?

A: Weekdays at 7:00 P.M.

B: What channel is it on?

A: Channel 9.

B: Is it *Wheel of Fortune*?

A: Yes, it is.

4 CONVERSATION STRATEGY: *Pausing*

A. 🎧 **PRONUNCIATION.** Listen and practice the expressions.

> I don't know.
> Let me see . . .

> Hmmm. Well,
> I guess . . .

> Let me think . . .

B. 🎧 **LISTEN and ADD.** Write the missing expressions. Then practice with a partner.

A: How many hours of TV do you usually watch every day?

B: _____ about two.

A: Interesting. How many TV shows do you watch regularly?

B: Regularly? _____ Three, I think.

5 TALKATHON: *TV questionnaire*

A. DISCUSS and DECIDE. Work with a partner. Read the questionnaire. Add two more questions.

Questions	Answers
1. How many hours of TV do you watch on a typical day?	
2. How many TV shows do you watch regularly?	
3. What are your two favorite TV stations or channels?	
4. What's the name of a very funny TV show?	
5.	
6.	

B. PAIR UP and TALK. Find a new partner. Ask your partner the questions. Write your partner's answers above.

C. REPORT. Join another pair. Report your partner's answers. Then discuss these questions.

1. Is there a TV station or channel everyone in your group likes?

2. Did two or more people name the same funny TV show?

3. What is the average number of hours that your group members watch TV?

4. What is the average number of TV shows people watch regularly?

Survey Central

The Most Popular Kinds of TV Shows

Rank	Brazil	Mexico	USA	Canada	Japan
1	National News	Local News	National and Local News	Movies	Weather
2	Local News	National News	Movies	National and Local News	Movies
3	International News	Action/ Adventure	Sitcoms	Sitcoms	National and Local News
4	Action/ Adventure	Sitcoms	Sports	Sports	Professional Baseball
5	Sitcoms	International News	Dramas	Biographies	Travel Shows

In My Opinion

The Sun   Letters to the Editor

Dear Editor:

These days, televisions are everywhere. I hate it! They're in restaurants, convenience stores, elevators, and buses. There is even a TV in my barbershop! Is there no escape? I don't watch TV at home, and I don't want to watch TV when I'm out. If you want to watch TV, just go home. Don't make me watch it, too!

Angry in Atlanta

TV Laughs

"*Dad, can you read?*"

READ ABOUT IT

A. Complete the sentences or answer the questions.

Survey Central
1. In all five countries, _____ is one of the three most popular kinds of TV shows.

2. In _____ countries, movies are one of the five most popular kinds of TV shows.

In My Opinion
3. What is the writer angry about?

TV Laughs
4. What is the message of the cartoon?

B. Compare answers with a partner.

TALK ABOUT IT

Discuss the questions with a partner.

Survey Central
1. Which countries seem most similar to each other?
2. Does anything in the survey surprise you?

In My Opinion
3. Do you agree with the writer? Why or why not?
4. Where is your favorite place to watch TV?

TV Laughs
5. Who watches more TV—you or your parents?

WRITE ABOUT IT

A. Take a survey. Ask some friends or family members about their five favorite kinds of TV shows. Make a chart like the one in Survey Central. Then answer the questions below.

Do the results surprise you? _____

Are the people in your survey more similar to or more different from each other?

_____

How are they similar or different? _____

B. Write about your survey.

EXAMPLE:

> I asked four friends about their five favorite kinds of TV shows. The results didn't surprise me. My friends are more similar than different. They all chose sitcoms and movies as two of their favorites.

Project Idea
TV Guide: Class Favorites
Make a schedule of your favorite TV shows. Include a short description of each show.

We're going to take a day trip.

1 VOCABULARY: *Vacation activities*

A. YOU FIRST. *Do you want to* _____ *on your next vacation?* Check (✓) yes or no.

1. do something fun

☐ yes ☐ no

2. visit relatives

☐ yes ☐ no

3. read something interesting

☐ yes ☐ no

4. do something dangerous

☐ yes ☐ no

5. hang out at the beach

☐ yes ☐ no

6. go somewhere new

☐ yes ☐ no

B. 🎧 PRONUNCIATION. Listen and practice the questions above.

C. PAIR UP and TALK. Interview a partner about the vacation activities above.

> Do you want to _____ on your next vacation?

> Hmmm . . . . Well, yes, I do.

> Where do you want to . . . ?

> Let's see. No, I don't.

> Why do you want to . . . ?

D. REPORT. Tell your classmates one thing your partner wants to do.

A. 🎧 **FIRST LISTENING.** What did these people do on their last vacation? Match.

1. Isabel   **2.** Jack   **3.** Masaki

a.   b.   c.

B. 🎧 **SECOND LISTENING.** Where is each person going to go on his or her next vacation? Why? Draw lines to match the person with a place and a reason.

Person	Place	Reason
Isabel	South Africa	To go somewhere new
Jack	Hawaii	To visit relatives
Masaki	Brazil	To go sightseeing and surfing
	Fiji	To go on a honeymoon

C. PAIR UP and TALK. *What's a good place for* _____ *?* Ask a partner.

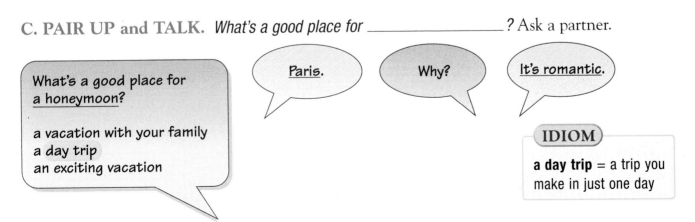

What's a good place for
a honeymoon?

a vacation with your family
a day trip
an exciting vacation

Paris.

Why?

It's romantic.

IDIOM

a day trip = a trip you
make in just one day

A. 🎧 **PRONUNCIATION.** Listen and practice the questions and answers.

What	**are** you	**going to do** this weekend?	I'm We're	**going to stay** home.
	is he	**going to do** tonight?	He's	**going to study**.
	are they	**going to do** tomorrow?	They're	**going to play** soccer.
Are you	**going to visit** friends?		Yes, No,	I **am**. we're **not**.

More Pronunciation Practice:

Reduced form of "going to"
Turn to page 85.

22

B. GET IT RIGHT. Complete the conversations. Then practice with a partner.

1. A: What _____ you _____ (do) on your next vacation?

B: We _____ (stay) home.

2. A: _____ you _____ (take) any day trips?

B: Yes, I _____. I _____ (drive) to the beach a few times.

3. A: When _____ your cousins _____ (visit)?

B: They _____ (visit) next month.

4. A: Where _____ he _____ (work) this summer?

B: He _____ (work) at a restaurant.

C. YOUR TURN. Work with a partner. Take turns.

Student A: Write down two things you're going to do next week. Don't show your partner! Give hints.
Student B: Guess what your partner is going to do.

Example: A: (Hint) I like jazz.

B: Are you going to go to a jazz concert?

A: No. I want a new CD.

B: Are you going to buy a jazz CD?

A: Yes!

I'm going to _____.
I'm going to _____.

A. 🎧 PRONUNCIATION. Listen and practice the questions.

> Who are you going to go with?

> Where are you going to stay?

> How are you going to get there?

> How long are you going to be away?

B. FINISH IT. Keep the conversation going. Write questions for "A." Then practice with a partner.

A: What are you going to do on your next vacation?

B: I'm going to take a bike tour.

A: _____?

B: _____.

A: _____?

B: _____.

A. TALK AROUND. Find classmates who are going to do the activities in the chart this weekend. Then ask questions to keep the conversation going.

Are you going to _____ this weekend?	Name	Details
go out of town		
do something with friends		
do something athletic		
visit relatives		
do a lot of reading		
do something unusual		

B. REPORT. Tell about one of your classmates.

> This weekend, Sandra is going to play tennis with a friend. They're going to play on Saturday afternoon at the tennis club.

Spotlight

For the adventure of a lifetime, go on one of these exciting GlobeTravel adventures!

Attention Animal Lovers!

Join us for a 100-mile walk across the Kenyan countryside. The trip takes 14 days and is for true animal lovers only. Walkers are sure to see many different animals including elephants, zebras, giraffes, and lions.

Calling All Space Tourists!

If you dream of being a cosmonaut, this vacation is for you. Participants attend a real cosmonaut training school in Moscow for one week. *Warning:* This experience is not for people who get sick on boats or airplanes!

Explorers' Dream Vacation!

This is the perfect vacation for adventurous people. You'll travel to the bottom of the ocean in a small submarine and explore a very old shipwreck from the 1800s.

Survey Central

Top Ten Countries That Foreign Tourists Visit

Country	Approximate Number of Tourists in Millions Every Year
France	75
United States	53
Spain	42
Italy	42
China	31
United Kingdom	25
Russia	23
Canada	21
Mexico	20
Germany	20

Vacation Laughs

"Gee, honey, this place has got everything."

READ ABOUT IT

A. Answer the questions.

Spotlight
1. What do the three trips have in common?

Survey Central
2. Approximately how many tourists go to France each year?
3. Which countries get approximately the same number of tourists each year?

Vacation Laughs
4. What places do you see in the cartoon?

B. Compare answers with a partner.

TALK ABOUT IT

Discuss the questions with a partner.

Spotlight
1. Which trip interests you? Why?

Survey Central
2. Are you surprised by any of these statistics? Why?
3. Which country in the table would you prefer to visit? Why?

Vacation Laughs
4. What do travelers *usually* mean when they say, "This place has everything"?

WRITE ABOUT IT

A. Make up an adventure trip on your own or in pairs. Make notes.

The location: _____

The main activities of the trip: _____

Why it is interesting to you: _____

The amount of time for the trip: _____

B. Imagine that you are going to go on the adventure trip. Write about it.

EXAMPLE:

My boyfriend and I love to dance, so we're going to go on a trip to Rio de Janeiro, Brazil. We're going to learn to do the samba. There are samba classes every morning, and at night there are trips to nightclubs so we can practice. This trip is for one week. I can't wait!

Project Idea
Brochure: Places to Visit
Design and illustrate a brochure about both well-known and unusual places to visit (and things to do) in your area.

Review of Units 1–3

1 INTERVIEW

A. How often do you do these things when you are on vacation? Complete the chart. Add your own ideas.

watch TV	take day trips	study English
go somewhere new	go sightseeing	do something with friends
hang out at the beach	visit relatives	listen to songs in English

always	sometimes	hardly ever	never

B. Interview a partner about vacations. Ask questions to keep the conversation going.

EXAMPLE:

A: Do you ever take day trips on your vacation?

B: No, hardly ever.

A: Oh, really? Why not?

2 INFORMATION GAP

Student A, turn to page 82. Student B, turn to page 83.

3 LISTENING

🎧 Listen to the questions and write your answers.

1. _____   4. _____

2. _____   5. _____

3. _____   6. _____

4 GAME

Play the game in groups of four.

A. Write your name on a small piece of paper.

B. Move your paper by flipping a coin.

 = one space   = two spaces

C. Each person in your group asks you a question about the topic. Answer your classmates' questions.

Question starters	
Are you going to . . . ?	Where . . . ?
Do you want to . . . ?	When . . . ?
Do you usually . . . ?	How long . . . ?
Do you ever . . . ?	Why . . . ?

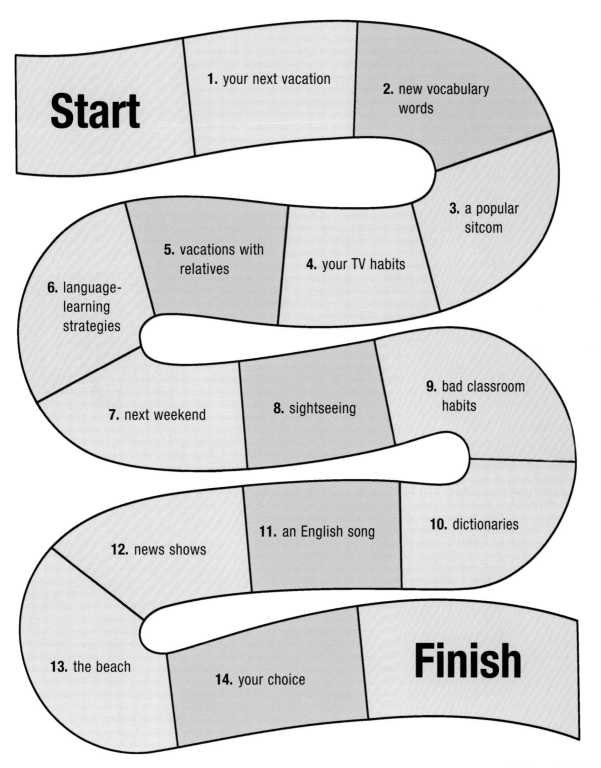

Start

1. your next vacation

2. new vocabulary words

3. a popular sitcom

4. your TV habits

5. vacations with relatives

6. language-learning strategies

7. next weekend

8. sightseeing

9. bad classroom habits

10. dictionaries

11. an English song

12. news shows

13. the beach

14. your choice

Finish

1 VOCABULARY: *Information sources*

A. YOU FIRST. *How do you usually* _____ *?* Check (✓) your answers.

How do you usually . . .?	I look in the newspaper.	I look online.	I watch TV.	I use the phone.	other
1. check the movie listings	☐	☐	☐	☐	☐
2. check a sports score	☐	☐	☐	☐	☐
3. find a phone number	☐	☐	☐	☐	☐
4. check a bus schedule	☐	☐	☐	☐	☐
5. check the weather forecast	☐	☐	☐	☐	☐

B. 🎧 **PRONUNCIATION.** Listen and practice the questions above.

C. PAIR UP and TALK. Ask a partner the questions.

> How do you usually check the movie listings?

> I usually look online, but sometimes I look in the newspaper.

D. REPORT. Tell your classmates one thing about your partner.

A. LOOK/THINK/GUESS. What is happening in these pictures?

Can you call me?

I'm returning your call.

B. 🎧 MODEL CONVERSATION. Listen and practice.

Sophie's voice mail:	Hi. I can't take your call right now, but you can leave a message at the beep.
Zack:	Hi, Sophie. This is Zack. Can you call me? I'm at home tonight. Thanks. Bye.
Zack's voice mail:	This is 734-0616. I can't talk right now. Please leave a message. Bye.
Sophie:	Hi, Zack. It's me—Sophie. I'm returning your call. I'm not sure what you wanted, but I'm about to go out so I can't talk to you tonight. Could you give me a ring tomorrow? Talk to you soon.

IDIOM

Give me a ring. = Call me on the telephone.

C. 🎧 ACTIVE LISTENING. Ben, Tim, and Meg call Zack. Listen to their messages on Zack's voice mail. Complete their messages below.

Name of Caller	Message
1. Ben	I need your new _____.
2. Tim	I need directions to _____.
3. Meg	I need the _____.

A. 🎧 PRONUNCIATION. Listen and practice the questions and answers.

QUESTIONS				ANSWERS			
Can	you	send	it by e-mail?	No,	I	**can't**.	
	I	get to	the airport by bus?	Yes,	you	**can**.	
Where	**can**	I	get	the airport bus?	You	**can**	get	it downtown.
When		you	meet	me?	I		meet	you tomorrow.

More Pronunciation Practice:

Reduced form of *"can"*
Turn to page 85.

B. GET IT RIGHT. Unscramble the questions. Then match them with the answers.

1. how / I / can / check the weather

   How can I check the weather ____ ?

2. I / can / get the bus / where

   _____ ?

3. call / can / I / you on your cell phone

   _____ ?

4. you / can / give me your e-mail address

   _____ ?

5. get to / can / the airport by train / I

   _____ ?

6. where / check my e-mail / can / I

   _____ ?

a. _____ You can go to an Internet café.

b. __1__ You can watch the Weather Channel.

c. _____ Sure. It's KathyZ at globelink dot com.

d. _____ No, you can't, but you can get there by bus.

e. _____ Sure. Do you have my cell phone number?

f. _____ At the downtown station.

C. YOUR TURN. Ask a partner a question for each situation.

Example: You want to contact your partner. *How can I contact you?*

1. You want to send your partner an e-mail.
2. You want to check a sports score.
3. You don't know your partner's phone number.

4. You want to meet your partner.
5. You want to buy train tickets.
6. You want to use your partner's cell phone.

A. 🎧 **PRONUNCIATION.** Listen and practice the questions.

Can you recommend a good website?

What's a good website?

B. 🎧 **LISTEN and ADD.** Write the missing expressions. Then practice with a partner.

A: I want to find a Canadian pen pal. _____ way to find one?

B: You can try the Internet.

A: That's a good idea. _____ website?

B: Hmmm. . . . I think there's a website called International Penpals dot com.

A: Okay, I'll try that. Thanks.

5 TALKATHON: *What's a good website?*

A. DISCUSS and DECIDE. With a partner, list things you can do on the Internet.

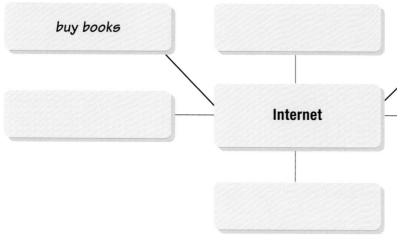

buy books

Internet

B. PAIR UP and TALK. Ask your partner about the list.

Example: A: Do you ever buy books on the Internet?

B: Yes, I do.

A: Can you recommend a good website?

B: Well, I really like Bookzone.

C. REPORT. Tell your classmates about a good website your partner recommended.

Cell Phone Laughs

"Would you mind talking to me for a while? I forgot my cell phone."

Headline News

New Phone Sends a Shock

A new kind of cell phone gives you a mild electric shock if you talk too loudly.

If you continue to talk loudly, the shock becomes stronger. "I want to give one to my brother," said one woman. "He is really annoying on cell phones."

OUCH!

Cell Phone Lounge Opens

Gabriel's Restaurant in New York City has a new room for cell phone users.

The room was created because so many customers complained about noisy cell phone users. The room seats twelve people. Now other customers can eat in peace.

Personal Stories

What's your experience with rude cell phone users?

" *I have a friend who talks on his cell phone a lot. He even took his cell phone to his wedding. During the wedding, his phone rang! He made a lot of people angry at his own wedding.* " —TERESA (Mexico)

" *One day I went to a classical music concert. During the concert, someone's cell phone rang. The person left the theater right away, but I could still hear her voice outside.* " —AKIKO (Japan)

" *Last week I had dinner at a restaurant with a friend. Her cell phone rang three times during our dinner, and each time she had a long conversation! I'm not going to go out with her again soon.* " —PAULO (Brazil)

READ ABOUT IT

A. Answer the questions.

Cell Phone Laughs
1. Why does this man want someone to talk to him?

Headline News
2. What can happen when you talk too loudly on some cell phones?
3. Where is the restaurant that has a special room for cell phone users?

Personal Stories
4. What do the three stories have in common?

B. Compare answers with a partner.

TALK ABOUT IT

Discuss the questions with a partner.

Cell Phone Laughs
1. What do you think the woman will say?

Headline News
2. What is a good way to stop people from talking on a cell phone too loudly?
3. Is it a good idea for restaurants to have a special room for cell phone users? Why or why not?
4. What other places do you think could have a special room for all phone users?

Personal Stories
5. Do you agree or disagree that these cell phone users are rude? Why?
6. Can you remember a time when a rude cell phone user annoyed you? What happened?

WRITE ABOUT IT

A. Think of a rude cell phone situation and make notes.

The location: _____

The reason it is rude: _____

A solution: _____

B. Write about your rude cell phone situation.

EXAMPLE:

I don't like it when I'm sitting on a bus or a train and a person near me is talking on a cell phone. It annoys me because I like to read or think about things. Why can't people just turn off their cell phones or use only text messaging when they are in public?

Project Idea
Visitors' Directory
Create a list of useful addresses, phone numbers, and websites for visitors to your area.

I have a great boss!

1 VOCABULARY: *Job characteristics*

A. YOU FIRST. *How important is* _____ *to you?* Write *extremely, very, somewhat,* or *not very* in the blanks.

1. a high salary

_____ important

2. a good boss

_____ important

3. lots of time off

_____ important

4. an easy commute

_____ important

5. job security

_____ important

6. interesting work

_____ important

B. 🎧 PRONUNCIATION. Listen and practice the questions above.

C. PAIR UP and TALK. Ask a partner the questions.

> How important is job security to you?

> Very important.

> That's interesting. I think job security is somewhat important.

D. REPORT. Tell your classmates one interesting thing your partner said.

2 LISTENING/GLOBAL INTERVIEWS: *Do you like your job?*

A. 🎧 **FIRST LISTENING.** John, Mia, and Deven are talking about their jobs. Write the number of the correct picture next to each person's name.

_____ John _____ Mia _____ Deven

1.

flight attendant

2.

chef

3.

computer programmer

4.

vet

5.

bookstore owner

6.

firefighter

B. 🎧 **SECOND LISTENING.** What do John, Mia, and Deven say about their jobs? Circle the correct word(s) in parentheses ( ).

1. John	I have a (nice/great) boss.	
	The work is (interesting/exciting).	
	The pay is (okay/not great).	
2. Mia	I get (a good salary/lots of time off).	
	I'm (never/hardly ever) bored.	
	I have (a great boss/good job security).	
3. Deven	I have pretty good (job security/vacations).	
	My (work/commute) is a breeze.	
	My salary is (great/not bad).	

> **IDIOM**
>
> **a breeze** = very easy

C. PAIR UP and TALK. Whose job would you prefer? Why?

3 LANGUAGE FOCUS: *Comparatives*

A. 🎧 **PRONUNCIATION.** Listen and practice the sentences and words.

> Doctors get **higher** salaries **than** vets.
> Vets work **longer** hours **than** doctors.
> A vet's job is **more dangerous than** a doctor's.
> A doctor's job is **more stressful than** a vet's.

long	→	long**er**
easy	→	eas**ier**
stressful	→	**more** stressful
good	→	**better**
bad	→	**worse**

More Pronunciation Practice:

Sentence stress
Turn to page 86.

B. GET IT RIGHT. Complete the questions. Then ask a partner the questions.

1. Who has a _____ job—a chef or a flight attendant? (hard)

2. Do you think a police officer's job is _____ than a firefighter's? (dangerous)

3. Do you think an architect gets a _____ salary than an engineer? (good)

4. Does a computer programmer get a _____ salary than a lawyer? (high)

5. Who has a _____ job—a bookstore owner or a clothing store owner? (interesting)

6. Who has an _____ job—a teacher of children or a teacher of adults? (easy)

7. Who has _____ vacations—a teacher or a doctor? (long)

8. Do you think a computer programmer's job is _____ than a lawyer's? (stressful)

C. YOUR TURN. With a partner, choose two famous people. Take turns asking questions about them. Use the adjectives in the box.

old	young	smart	rich	exciting	popular
funny	crazy	famous	happy	good-looking	interesting

> Who is <u>older</u>, <u>Bill Gates</u> or <u>Britney Spears</u>?

> <u>Bill Gates</u>. Who is <u>better-looking</u>?

4 CONVERSATION STRATEGY: *Expanding your answer*

A. 🎧 **MODEL CONVERSATIONS.** Listen and practice the conversations.

1. A: Would you rather be a boss or an employee?

B: I'd rather be a boss. The salary is higher, and the work is more interesting.

2. A: Would you rather be a boss or an employee?

B: I'd rather be an employee. The work is easier, and the hours are shorter.

B. FINISH IT. Complete the conversation. Then practice with a partner.

A: Would you rather be a boss or an employee?

B: I'd rather be _____. _____.

5 CONVERSATION MAP: *What would you rather be?*

A. YOU FIRST. Think of three jobs that you like. Write each job in an orange space below.

B. PAIR UP and TALK. Ask about the jobs below. Write your partner's answers on the lines. Remember to expand your answer.

Example:
A: Would you rather be a travel agent or an accountant?
B: I'd rather be a travel agent. The job is more interesting. It's also easier.
A: Okay. Would you rather be a travel agent or _____?

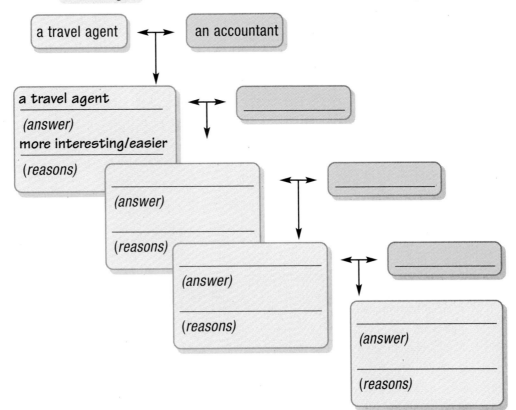

C. REPORT. Tell your classmates about your partner's job preferences.

Work Laughs

"Could you give me a little push?"

Top Five List

Here are the top five complaints that employees make about their bosses:

Bad bosses . . .

1. never listen to their employees;
2. change their minds often;
3. give unclear instructions;
4. tell you your weaknesses but not your strengths;
5. steal their employees' ideas.

Personal Stories

What is your unusual job?

I am a trend-spotter. That means I tell businesses about new styles and fashions. For example, I tell clothing manufacturers about fashions that are becoming "hot." To get information, I talk to people, watch TV and movies, and go shopping. I love it!

—YON-MI (Korea)

I love to travel, and now that's all I do. I work for a big hotel chain. My job is to stay in different hotels for a few days and write reports about my experiences. I stay in hotels all over the world. This is my dream job!

—MARK (UK)

I'm an actor. It's hard to get jobs in the theater, so I act in hospitals. I play the role of a patient for medical students. They practice on me. It's not easy. I have to learn all about each illness for my "performance." It's not Broadway, but I enjoy it because I am acting and because I am helping students become better doctors.

—DAMIEN (U.S.)

READ ABOUT IT

A. Answer the questions.

Work Laughs
1. Why is the man asking his wife for a push?

Top Five List
2. What do bad bosses do?
3. What do bad bosses *not* do?

Personal Stories
4. What do Yon-Mi, Damien, and Mark love to do?

B. Compare answers with a partner.

TALK ABOUT IT

Discuss the questions with a partner.

Work Laughs
1. Do you ever feel like this man? When and why?

Top Five List
2. Do you know any bad bosses? Do you agree with the top five list?
3. What do *good* bosses do and not do? Make a top five list for good bosses.

Personal Stories
4. Do any of these jobs sound fun to you? Why?
5. What is *your* dream job?

WRITE ABOUT IT

A. Make notes on one of the jobs on page 32 or another job of your choice.

The job: _____

The things you like about the job: _____

The things you don't like about the job: _____

B. Write about the job.

EXAMPLE:

> I think the trend-spotter job sounds fun. I'm interested in fashion, and I love shopping, watching TV, and going to movies. However, the job sounds stressful. What if you make a mistake and tell people the wrong thing?

Project Idea
Directory of Unusual Jobs
Research unusual jobs on the Internet. Write a description of one job. Compile the descriptions into a directory of unusual jobs.

6 She's really outgoing!

1 VOCABULARY: *Personal characteristics*

A. YOU FIRST. *Are you* _____ *or* _____ ? Check (✓) your answers.

1.

☐ **outgoing**   ☐ **quiet**

2.

☐ **messy**   ☐ **neat**

3.

☐ **lazy**   ☐ **hardworking**

4.

☐ **serious**   ☐ **funny**

B. 🎧 **PRONUNCIATION.** Listen and practice the questions above.

C. PAIR UP and TALK. Ask a partner the questions.

> Are you outgoing or quiet?

> I'm outgoing with friends, but I'm quiet with people I don't know.

D. REPORT. Tell one way you and your partner are alike and one way you are different.

> I'm _____, but my partner is _____.

A. 🎧 **FIRST LISTENING.** How many brothers and sisters does each person have? Write the number. What is his or her position in the family? Check (✓) *oldest, middle, youngest,* or *only child.*

Person	# of brothers	# of sisters	Position in family	
Abby			☐ oldest child ☐ middle child	☐ youngest child ☐ only child
Rita			☐ oldest child ☐ middle child	☐ youngest child ☐ only child
Ken			☐ oldest child ☐ middle child	☐ youngest child ☐ only child

B. 🎧 **SECOND LISTENING.** What do they say about their brothers and sisters? Circle the correct word(s) in parentheses ( ).

1. Abby is (more outgoing/more serious) than her sister.

2. Abby is (messier/neater) than her sister.

3. Rita is (messier/neater) than her older brother.

4. Rita is (lazier/more hardworking) than her older brother.

5. Ken's (oldest brother/middle brother) is the quietest person in his family.

6. Ken's (oldest brother/middle brother) is the funniest person in his family.

Now look at the photos. Can you find Abby, Rita, and Ken?

C. PAIR UP and TALK. Ask a partner about his or her family.

> How many brothers and sisters do you have?

> I have _____ _____.

> How are you different from your family members?

> Well, let me see . . . . _____.

3 LANGUAGE FOCUS: *Comparatives and superlatives*

A. 🎧 **PRONUNCIATION.** Listen and practice the questions and words.

	Adjective	Comparative	Superlative
Is your mother **younger than** your father? Who's **the youngest** person in your family?	young old	younger older	the youngest the oldest
Who's **more outgoing**—your mother or your sister? Who's **the most outgoing** person in your family?	funny outgoing	funnier more outgoing	the funniest the most outgoing
Are you a **better** cook **than** your son? Who's **the best** cook in your family?	good bad	better worse	the best the worst

*More
Pronunciation
Practice:*

Intonation of "or" questions
Turn to page 87.

B. GET IT RIGHT. Complete the questions. Then ask a partner the questions.

1. Who's _____ person in your family? (young)

2. Are you _____ person in your family? (funny)

3. Are you _____ person in your family? (tall)

4. Who's _____ person in your family? (serious)

5. Who's _____ person in your family? (old)

6. Who's _____ cook in your family? (good)

7. Are you _____ person in your family? (relaxed)

8. Are you _____ person in your family? (messy)

C. YOUR TURN. Write questions about your classmates. Ask a partner your questions.

> Who's the <u>most athletic</u> person in the class?

> I think _____ _____ is.

> Who's the <u>funniest</u> person in the class?

> It's probably _____.

CONVERSATION STRATEGY: *Showing you are interested*

A. 🎧 **PRONUNCIATION.** Listen and practice the expressions.

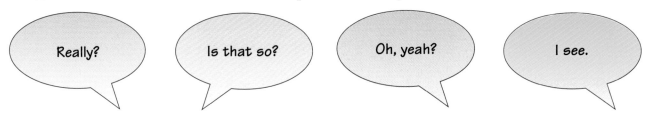

Really?   Is that so?   Oh, yeah?   I see.

B. 🎧 **LISTEN and ADD.** Write the missing expressions. Then practice with a partner.

A: Who's the funniest person in your family?

B: Hmmm…. I guess my sister Kate is. She's a riot.

A: _____. Is she older or younger than you?

B: She's ten years older.

A: _____. That's a lot older.

> **IDIOM**
>
> **a riot** = a very funny person

---

5 **TWO-MINUTE INTERVIEWS:** *The most interesting person*

A. YOU FIRST. Choose an interesting person in your family. Make notes below.

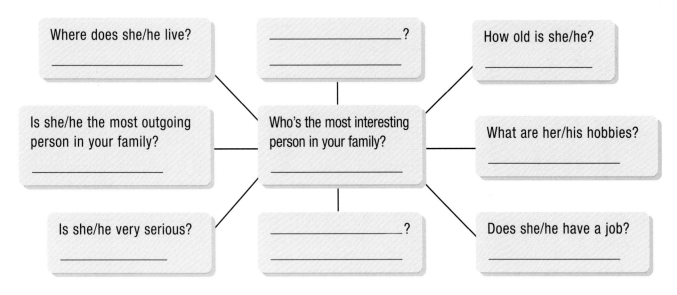

Where does she/he live?
_____

_____?
_____

How old is she/he?
_____

Is she/he the most outgoing person in your family?
_____

Who's the most interesting person in your family?
_____

What are her/his hobbies?
_____

Is she/he very serious?
_____

_____?
_____

Does she/he have a job?
_____

B. TALK AROUND. Interview a partner for two minutes. Remember to show interest. Then interview two more people.

Who's the most interesting person in your family?

My uncle Fred is.

I see. Where does he live?

C. REPORT. Tell your classmates something interesting about a classmate's relative.

Headline News

Birth Order May Affect Career Choice

Did you know that . . .

- Almost all of the U.S. presidents were the first-born child in their families?
- All but two of the first astronauts sent into space were first-borns, and the other two were "only children"?

Are these just coincidences? Some researchers think they aren't. In fact, recent studies suggest that a child's place in the family birth order may affect the career she or he chooses.

Oldest children are typically successful and are natural leaders. Business executives and world leaders are often the oldest child in their families.

Maybe they are good leaders because of their experience taking care of younger brothers and sisters.

Middle children are usually more relaxed than oldest children. They often help their older and younger siblings to get along, so they are good at jobs that require cooperation, negotiation, and teamwork.

Youngest children often become artists, actors, comedians, and salespeople. These are ideal occupations for them because they are typically creative, friendly, and funny.

Family Laughs

"Am I the smart one and you're the pretty one or is it the other way around?"

In My Opinion

"My zodiac sign is Libra, so I'm outgoing and social. I was born in the year of the sheep, so I'm quiet and shy. My favorite animals are cats, so I like to stay home. My favorite color is orange, so I love to go to parties. How can all of this be true? It seems like there are a hundred ways to analyze personalities. If you ask me, they're all superstitions!"

—KAREN (U.S.)

READ ABOUT IT

A. Answer the questions.

Headline News
1. What does this article say about birth order and career choice?
2. According to this article, what are typical characteristics of oldest children, middle children, and youngest children?

Family Laughs
3. Why is the woman asking her sister this question?

In My Opinion
4. What are some ways to analyze personalities? What does the writer think of them?

B. Compare answers with a partner.

TALK ABOUT IT

Discuss the questions with a partner.

Headline News
1. Do you agree with the article? Why or why not?
2. What do you think are typical characteristics of an only child?

Family Laughs
3. If you have a sibling, did your parents ever make comparisons between you? What did they say? How did you feel about it?

In My Opinion
4. Do you agree with the writer? Do you know other ways to analyze personalities?

WRITE ABOUT IT

A. Make notes about your family.

What is the birth order in your family? _____

Is the article true for your family? Why or why not? _____

B. Write about birth order in your family.

EXAMPLE:

The description in the article is not true for my family. There are two children in my family—me and my older sister. My sister is very outgoing and funny. People like her, and she has lots of friends. She was not a very good student, and now she is an actress. I am not a typical youngest child, because I am serious and hardworking. I plan to be a lawyer when I finish university.

Project Idea
Collage: Who am I?
Create a collage that describes you: your personality, your interests, your family, where you live, what you do. Use pictures and English words and phrases.

Review of Units 4–6

1 ROLE PLAY

A. Make up a message for your voice mail.

B. Take turns as Student A and Student B.

Student A: Call Student B on the telephone.

Student B: You aren't home. Say your voice mail message.

Student A: Leave a message. Use the ideas in the box to help you.

> You want to meet downtown tomorrow.
> You want to find out the homework assignment.
> You can't meet downtown tomorrow.
> You can't find a friend's cell phone number.

C. Perform your role play for your classmates.

2 INTERVIEW

A. Write at least three items in each column.

dangerous jobs	funny actors	beautiful places	good singers	interesting websites

B. Interview a partner about his or her chart.

What are some dangerous jobs?

Which job is more dangerous— _____ or _____?

Which job is the most dangerous?

Who are some funny actors?

Who is funnier— _____ or _____?

Who is the funniest actor?

A. 🎧 Listen to the conversation. Write four things about Lauren's sister.

1. _____

2. _____

3. _____

4. _____

B. Share your list with a partner.

4 GAME

Divide into teams of three or four students. Two teams play together.

1. **Team A:** Choose an item from the grid.

2. **Team B:** Ask a question about the item. Team A answers.

3. **Team A:** Ask a question about the item. Team B answers.

4. When one team can't think of a question, the other team gets a point.

5. **Team B:** Choose an item from the grid. Repeat steps two through four.

6. Continue playing until all of the items have been chosen. The team with the most points wins.

EXAMPLE:

neat

Team A: We choose **neat.**

Team B: Who is the **neatest** person in the class?

Team A: _____. What is the opposite of **neat?**

Team B: Messy. Who is **neater**—_____ or _____ ?

Team A: _____. What does **neat** mean?

cell phone	voice mail	the weather forecast	the Internet
a good boss	job security	a dangerous job	funny
oldest child	a vet	a high salary	quiet

7

I'm pretty swamped.

1 VOCABULARY: *School subjects*

A. YOU FIRST. Check (✓) your answers to one of these questions:

If you **are** a student: *Are you taking a/an _____ course?*
If you **aren't** a student: *Did you take a/an _____ course in school?*

1. history ☐ yes ☐ no

2. literature ☐ yes ☐ no

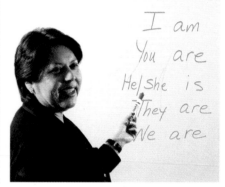

3. foreign language ☐ yes ☐ no

4. science ☐ yes ☐ no

5. math ☐ yes ☐ no

6. art ☐ yes ☐ no

B. 🎧 PRONUNCIATION. Listen and practice the questions above.

C. PAIR UP and TALK. Interview a partner about school courses.

A: Are you taking <u>a math</u> course?	A: Did you take <u>an art</u> course in school?
B: Yes, I am. I'm taking <u>calculus</u>.	B: Yes, I did. I took <u>sculpture</u>.
A: Do you like it?	A: Really? Did you like it?

Courses
European history
British literature
Russian
biology
chemistry
algebra
physics
painting

D. REPORT. Tell your classmates one thing about your partner.

A. LOOK/THINK/GUESS. What do you think Zack and his father are talking about?

B. 🎧 **MODEL CONVERSATION.** Listen and practice.

Zack's father:	How are your courses this semester?
Zack:	They're great, Dad. I'm pretty swamped, though!
Zack's father:	Really? What are you studying?
Zack:	Well, I'm taking a history course.
Zack's father:	That's wonderful. Everyone should study history. What kind of history are you taking? Ancient history?
Zack:	Not exactly. It's more like film history.
Zack's father:	Film history? That doesn't sound very serious.
Zack:	It is, Dad. I'm learning a lot.

> **IDIOM**
>
> **swamped** = very busy

C. 🎧 **ACTIVE LISTENING.** What other courses is Zack taking? What is Zack's opinion of each course? What is his father's opinion? Check (✓) your answers.

Subject	Course	Zack's opinion	His father's opinion
Foreign language	☐ Spanish ☐ Chinese ☐ Greek	☐ is boring ☐ isn't too boring	☐ is useful ☐ isn't useful
Science	☐ Chemistry ☐ Food science ☐ Biology	☐ is practical ☐ isn't practical	☐ is a science ☐ isn't a science

3 LANGUAGE FOCUS: *"Should" and "have to"*

A. 🎧 **PRONUNCIATION.** Listen and practice the statements.

Use *should/shouldn't* for **opinions**.

University students	**should**	study every weekend.
Parents	**shouldn't**	do their children's homework.

Use *have to/don't have to* for **facts**.

In the U.S., children	**have to**	go to school until age 16.
At my school, students	**don't have to**	wear a uniform.

More Pronunciation Practice:

Syllable stress
Turn to page 87.

B. GET IT RIGHT.

Give the facts. Write *have to* or *don't have to*.

In my country,

1. most university students _____ wear uniforms.

2. high school students _____ study a foreign language.

3. students _____ take entrance examinations to enter university.

4. children _____ go to school until age 18.

Give your opinion. Write *should* or *shouldn't*.

In my opinion,

5. university students _____ wear uniforms.

6. high school students _____ study a foreign language.

7. students _____ take entrance examinations to enter university.

8. children _____ go to school until age 18.

C. YOUR TURN. With a partner, make a list for each category. Then tell your ideas to another pair.

In our English class, we . . .

have to	don't have to	should	shouldn't

Example: We don't have to be quiet.

A. 🎧 **PRONUNCIATION.** Listen and practice the expressions.

In my opinion, students should . . .

I think high school students should . . .

I feel strongly that students should . . .

I don't think students should . . .

B. 🎧 **LISTEN and ADD.** Write the missing expressions. Then practice with a partner.

A: I think high school students should work part time. What do you think?

B: _____ that they _____ work.

A: Really? Why?

B: Because they have to study, and they don't have time to work.

A: I don't agree. _____ high school students _____ have part-time jobs.

B: Why?

A: Because _____ students _____ learn to be independent.

5 TALKATHON: *What should I do?*

A. DISCUSS and DECIDE. Read the problems below. Then, with a partner, think of three more problems. They can be real or imagined.

Examples:

"Our teachers give us a lot of homework, especially math. I have a part-time job, so I have to study late at night. I'm always tired. What should I do?"

"One of my co-workers plays computer games at work. He doesn't finish his work, so I have to help him. It's very annoying. What should I do?"

Problems:

1. _____ .

2. _____ .

3. _____ .

B. TALK AROUND. Tell your problems to a classmate and ask for advice. Then ask two more classmates for advice.

What should I do?

I think you should tell your boss about your co-worker.

C. REPORT. Tell your classmates the most interesting piece of advice.

Education Laughs

Survey Central

This table shows the age at which students have to start studying a foreign language in ten countries.

Country	Students' starting age	First foreign language(s)
Austria	6	English
Brazil	11–12	English
Czech Republic	9	English and German
Denmark	10	English
Germany	8	English or other*
Italy	8	English
Luxembourg	6–7	German and French
Morocco	9	French
Spain	8	English
Thailand	6	English

* French, Spanish, Russian, Italian, Turkish.

Daily Investigation

The Sun

An Unusual School

I thought that these days you could only find cowboys in the movies, but I was wrong. In fact, there's even a school for people who want to be cowboys. It's called the Arizona Cowboy College, and men and women from all over the world attend this school. It is not for people looking for a fun vacation; it's for people who are serious about learning to be cowboys. The course lasts six days and is dangerous and difficult. Students learn how to take care of cows and horses and how to run a ranch. Of course, students also learn how to ride horses. A typical day starts at sunrise and ends after dark. Students need to be prepared to work, eat, and sleep under the stars.

READ ABOUT IT

A. Answer the questions.

Education Laughs
1. The boy's parents are wearing barrels. Why don't they have money for clothes?

Survey Central
2. What is the earliest age that children start studying a foreign language?
3. What languages other than English do children study?

Daily Investigation
4. How long is the Arizona Cowboy College course?
5. What two adjectives describe this course?

B. Compare answers with a partner.

TALK ABOUT IT

Discuss the questions with a partner.

Education Laughs
1. Who do you think should pay for university—the government or the student's family? Why?

Survey Central
2. When did you start studying a foreign language? Which language?
3. What do you think is the best age to start studying a foreign language? Why?

Daily Investigation
4. What kinds of people do you think go to Cowboy College?
5. Does this course interest you? Why or why not?

WRITE ABOUT IT

A. Design a school similar to the Arizona Cowboy College. Make notes.

The skill: _____

Who the school is for: _____

The length of the course: _____

A few of the classes: _____

B. Write about your school.

EXAMPLE:

> My school is called Cassie's Cake-Making School. This school is for people who like to bake cakes or for people who work in a bakery or restaurant. The course lasts ten days. There are classes on cake decorating, baking for large groups of people, and making wedding cakes. The course is hard work but lots of fun.

Project Idea
Catalog:
Unusual Schools

Use the schools you wrote about in "Write About It" to create an "unusual school catalog." Include information about requirements and schedule.

8

It's easy come, easy go.

1 VOCABULARY: *Spending habits*

A. YOU FIRST. *Did you* _____ *last week?* Check (✓) *yes* or *no*. If you check *yes*, answer the follow-up question.

1. spend any money on clothes

☐ yes   ☐ no

What did you buy? _____

2. use a credit card

☐ yes   ☐ no

Where? _____

3. buy a gift

☐ yes   ☐ no

What? _____

4. buy anything in a department store

☐ yes   ☐ no

Which store? _____

5. buy anything you didn't really need

☐ yes   ☐ no

What? _____

6. put any money in the bank

☐ yes   ☐ no

When? _____

B. 🎧 PRONUNCIATION. Listen and practice the questions above.

C. PAIR UP and TALK. Ask a partner the questions. Ask follow-up questions.

> Did you spend any money on clothes last week?

> Yes, I did.

> You did? What did you buy?

> I bought a shirt.

D. REPORT. Tell your classmates one thing about your partner.

A. 🎧 **FIRST LISTENING.** Four people are talking about their spending habits. For each person, check (✓) *spender* or *saver*.

1. Julie

☐ spender   ☐ saver

2. Pedro

☐ spender   ☐ saver

3. Nora

☐ spender   ☐ saver

4. Mike

☐ spender   ☐ saver

B. 🎧 **SECOND LISTENING.** Listen and match each person to one or more sentences.

1. Julie

2. Pedro

3. Nora

4. Mike

a. I like to do both.

b. It's easy come, easy go.

c. I love to shop until I drop.

d. As soon as I get some money, I spend it.

e. I love to spend money.

f. I'm always broke.

g. My friends probably say I'm cheap!

h. I like to save money.

> **IDIOMS**
>
> **It's easy come, easy go.** = I usually spend money when I have it.
>
> **shop until I drop** = shop until I'm very tired

C. PAIR UP and TALK. Ask your partner *"Are you a spender or a saver?"* Remember to expand your answer.

Are you a spender or a saver?

I'm a _____. I . . .

A. 🎧 **PRONUNCIATION.** Listen and practice the questions and statements.

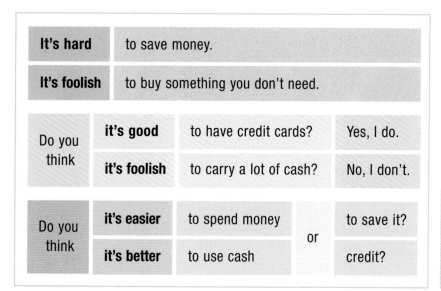

It's hard	to save money.		
It's foolish	to buy something you don't need.		

Do you think	it's good	to have credit cards?	Yes, I do.
	it's foolish	to carry a lot of cash?	No, I don't.

Do you think	it's easier	to spend money	*or*	to save it?
	it's better	to use cash		credit?

More Pronunciation Practice:

Embedded questions Turn to page 88.

It's easier	to spend money.
It's better	to use cash.

B. GET IT RIGHT. Choose an adjective to complete the questions. (More than one adjective is possible.) Then ask a partner the questions.

easy/easier	hard/harder	smart/smarter
good/better	important/more important	foolish/more foolish

1. Do you think it's _____ to spend money?

2. Do you think it's _____ to spend money or to save it?

3. Do you think it's _____ to pay your bills?

4. Do you think it's _____ to have a lot of credit cards?

5. Do you think it's _____ to earn money or to spend it?

6. Do you think it's _____ to spend money on travel?

7. Do you think it's _____ to lend your friends money?

8. Do you think it's _____ to borrow money or to lend it?

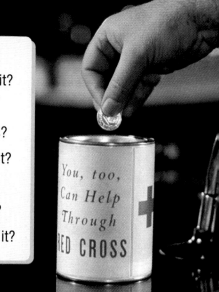

You, too, Can Help Through RED CROSS

C. YOUR TURN. Ask a partner questions about the items below.

1. ask questions in English class

2. give money to charity

3. live in the city or in the suburbs

4. be a man or a woman

5. travel by train or by bus

> Do you think it's good to give money to charity?

> Yes, I do.

4 CONVERSATION STRATEGY: *Reaching a compromise*

A. 🎧 **PRONUNCIATION.** Listen and practice the expressions.

> I like that idea because . . .

> That makes sense to me.

> Why don't we . . . ?

> I'd rather . . .

B. 🎧 **LISTEN and ADD.** Write the missing expressions. Then practice with a partner.

A: I think we should stay at the Palm Inn. It's nice, and it's not very expensive.

B: Actually, _____ stay at a nicer hotel.

A: _____ stay one night at the Royal Palace and two nights at the Budget Bungalow?

B: _____.

5 TALKATHON: *A trip to Palm Tree Island*

A. DISCUSS and DECIDE. Work in groups of four. You are going to Palm Tree Island for three days and two nights. You all have to stay in the same hotel and do the same things. Each person can spend 18 points. Decide how to spend your points.

Places to Stay	Things to Do	
The Royal Palace Hotel — 4 points per night	Go to a nightclub — 3 points per night	Take a helicopter ride — 4 points (half day)
The Palm Inn — 3 points per night	Go sailing — 3 points (full day)	Go shopping — 4 points (half day)
The Budget Bungalow — 2 points per night	Swim with dolphins — 5 points (half day)	Rent a motorbike — 2 points (full day)

B. REPORT. Tell your classmates about your plans.

Money Laughs

"Let's face it—man's best friend is money."

Headline News

The Sun

Bartering is back!

Before the invention of money, people didn't buy things; they bartered—that is, exchanged products and services. These days, bartering is becoming very popular again. Both small and large companies barter. In Asia, companies barter approximately $90 billion a year of products or services. In the U.S., 250,000 businesses use bartering instead of money exchanges some of the time. Bartering helps companies save money because they pay for things with their own products or services. For example, a hotel needs beds. They can offer free rooms to a furniture company in exchange for new beds. It's a win–win situation for everyone.

Survey Central

Winning the lottery is the best thing that can happen to you, right? Wrong! Actually, winning the lottery can cause lots of problems. Here are some common complaints of lottery winners:

1. Most winners quit their jobs, but they get bored because they have too much free time.

2. Friends expect you to pay for everything.

3. People and organizations always ask you for money.

4. It's hard to know who your friends are and who likes you only for your money.

5. Spouses and partners argue about how to spend the money.

6. It's common to worry about people robbing you.

7. Most winners buy bigger, more expensive houses. However, they often don't have much in common with their new neighbors.

8. Lottery winners sometimes feel guilty about suddenly being rich.

READ ABOUT IT

A. Answer the questions.

Money Laughs

1. There's a saying: "A dog is a man's best friend." Do the dogs agree or disagree?

Headline News

2. What is bartering?
3. How does bartering help companies?

Survey Central

4. Why do lottery winners sometimes get bored?
5. Why do lottery winners argue with spouses or partners?

B. Compare answers with a partner.

TALK ABOUT IT

Discuss the questions with a partner.

Money Laughs

1. Do you agree that money is the most important thing to most people?
2. Is having money very important to you? Why?

Headline News

3. What products or services could you barter?

Survey Central

4. Which of these complaints are reasonable? Which are silly?
5. Can you think of other possible problems of winning a lottery?

WRITE ABOUT IT

A. You won the lottery! Make notes on what you are going to do.

How much money: _____

Your plans: _____

Any worries? _____

B. Write about your plans.

EXAMPLE:

> I won ten million dollars in the lottery last week. I still can't believe it! I'm going to quit my job and travel for the rest of my life. I'm also going to give some of the money to charities. I'm going to hire a chef so I never have to cook again! My only worry is that I'm going to miss my friends at work.

Project Idea
Money Survey

Create a survey to find out how people spend their money and how they feel about money. Interview as many people as you can. Compile the results.

1 VOCABULARY: *Personal characteristics*

A. YOU FIRST. *How important is it for a couple to have the same* _____?
Write *very important*, *somewhat important*, or *not very important* under each picture.

1. taste in movies
_____

2. blood type
_____

3. amount of money
_____

4. level of education
_____

5. interests
_____

6. religion
_____

B. 🎧 PRONUNCIATION. Listen and practice the questions above.

C. PAIR UP and TALK. Discuss these questions with a partner.

1. What are the two most important things for couples to have in common?

2. What are the two least important things for couples to have in common?

> I think the two most important things for couples to have in common are <u>blood type</u> and <u>amount of money</u>.

> Really? I think
> _____.

D. REPORT. Tell your classmates one thing you and your partner agree on.

A. LOOK/THINK/GUESS. Do you think Dan and Denise will go out again? Why or why not?

B. 🎧 MODEL CONVERSATION. Listen and practice.

Sophie: Hi, Dan. How was your date with my friend Denise? I know you two have a lot in common. Did you hit it off?

Dan: Oh, it was okay, I guess.

Sophie: Just "okay"? Denise is great!

Dan: Yeah, but she likes to talk . . . a lot.

Sophie: Well, so do you.

Dan: I know, but I'm funny.

Sophie: Well, so is Denise.

Dan: She is? Do you think she's funnier than I am?

Sophie: I didn't say that. But maybe you're just too much alike.

> (IDIOM)
>
> **hit it off** = like someone very much the first time you meet

C. 🎧 ACTIVE LISTENING. Listen to two more conversations. Are the people alike or different? Check (✔). How are they alike or different?

Conversation 1

Liz and Lucy are ☐ alike. ☐ different.

How? _____

_____

Conversation 2

Zack and Meg are ☐ alike. ☐ different.

How? _____

_____

3 LANGUAGE FOCUS: *"So," "Neither"*

A. 🎧 **PRONUNCIATION.** Listen and practice the conversations.

A: I'm tired. B: **So am** I.	A: I'm not bored. B: **Neither am** I.	A: I like tennis. B: **So do** I.	A: I don't like tennis. B: **Neither do** I.
A: She's tired. B: **So is** he.	A: She's not bored. B: **Neither is** he.	A: He likes tennis. B: **So does** she.	A: She doesn't like tennis. B: **Neither does** he.

More Pronunciation Practice:
Reduced form of "does he," "does she"
Turn to page 88.

B. GET IT RIGHT. Complete the conversations with *so* or *neither* and *am, is, do,* or *does.* Then practice with a partner.

1. A: I am never late to class.
   B: _Neither am_ I.

2. A: I sometimes daydream in class.
   B: _____ I.

3. A: I like game shows.
   B: _____ he.

4. A: I'm not tired.
   B: _____ she.

5. A: I'm taking an art class.
   B: _____ I.

6. A: He doesn't smoke.
   B: _____ she.

7. A: She loves jazz.
   B: _____ I.

8. A: He's always on time.
   B: _____ she.

9. A: She isn't neat.
   B: _____ I.

10. A: He's not very talkative.
   B: _____ she.

C. YOUR TURN. Work with a partner. Take turns.

Student A: Choose a word from the box and make a sentence with it.

Student B: Respond with *neither* or *so.*

Example:

> I don't like soap operas.

> Neither does my sister.

funny	outgoing
tired	late
quiet	soap operas
classical music	computer

4 CONVERSATION STRATEGY: *Ending a conversation*

A. 🎧 **PRONUNCIATION.** Listen and practice the expressions.

> Well, I have to go.

> Nice talking to you.

> Good talking to you.

B. 🎧 **LISTEN and ADD.** Write the missing expressions. Then practice with a partner.

A: Tom! How are you?

B: I'm fine. It's great to see you! How's Eric?

A: Oh, he's fine. He's in Spain right now.

B: Really! What's he doing there?

A: He's camping with friends.

B: That sounds like fun! _____

A: _____

5 TWO-MINUTE INTERVIEWS: *What do you have in common?*

A. YOU FIRST. Complete the sentences for each category.

TV SHOWS

I like (to) _____ .

I sometimes watch _____ .

I don't _____ .

VACATIONS

I like (to) _____ .

I usually _____ .

I don't _____ .

STUDY HABITS

I like to _____ .

I sometimes _____ .

I don't usually _____ .

FAMILY

I have _____ .

I _____ with my family.

I don't usually _____ with my family.

B. TALK AROUND. Interview a partner for two minutes and find two things you have in common. Remember to end the conversation. Then find a new partner.

> Do you like to watch sitcoms?

> Yes, I do. Do you?

> Yes, I do.

> Well, I have to go. Nice talking to you.

> Nice talking to you.

C. REPORT. Tell your classmates what you have in common with one of your partners.

Daily Investigation

Do Opposites Attract?

The saying "opposites attract" is true for magnets but not necessarily for people. A new study shows that people look for mates who are similar to them. For example, athletic people prefer other athletic people. In the study, people rated themselves in terms of these characteristics: how much money they have, their social class, how loyal they are, and their appearance. The same people then rated the importance of each of these characteristics in a mate. This study helps to explain why couples who are similar get along better than couples who are different. ♥

Romance Laughs

"I don't care if she is a tape dispenser. I love her."

Personal Opinions

We asked people to compare romantic customs in their country and the U.S. Here's what they said:

- *Americans often show their feelings openly, but Chinese prefer to show their feelings only in private.*
- *Americans like to say "I love you" and call each other words like "honey" and "sweetie." Chinese people don't say "I love you" often, and they call each other by indirect names such as "mother or father of our children."*

—HSUI-MEI (China)

- *Both Americans and Mexicans like to have special dinners on a date. However, Americans like to eat out in restaurants, and Mexicans prefer to have homemade dinners.*
- *Both Americans and Mexicans like to give flowers as gifts, but Mexicans especially like to give their loved ones red roses.*

—LORENA (Mexico)

READ ABOUT IT

A. Answer the questions.

Daily Investigation
1. Which kinds of couples stay together longer—ones with more differences or more similarities?
2. What four characteristics did people rate?

Romance Laughs
3. Why does the snail love the tape dispenser?

Personal Opinions
4. Which country's romantic customs are more similar to those in the U.S.—China's or Mexico's?

B. Compare answers with a partner.

TALK ABOUT IT

Discuss the questions with a partner.

Daily Investigation
1. Do you agree with the article? Why or why not?
2. Which of the four characteristics is most important to you in a mate?

Romance Laughs
3. Do you know a couple in which the two people are very different from each other? How are they different?

Personal Opinions
4. Which way of being romantic fits you best?

WRITE ABOUT IT

A. Compare yourself with a good friend. Make notes on your similarities and differences.

Your friend's name: _____

Differences: _____

Similarities: _____

B. Write about your relationship.

EXAMPLE:

My friend's name is Wen De. We're very different, but we're very good friends. Wen De loves to play sports, but I prefer to watch them. I also like to read and to play chess, but Wen De doesn't like to do those things. However, we both love music. We often listen to CDs and go to concerts together.

Project Idea
Guide: Tips for Romance
Make a list of suggestions ("tips") for the best ways to show you like someone. Compile the tips into a guide about how to be romantic.

Review of Units 7–9

1 AGREE/DISAGREE

A. Check (✓) *agree* or *disagree*.

	agree	disagree
1. It's difficult to write in English.	_____	_____
2. It's easy to do well in high school.	_____	_____
3. It's important to learn more than one language.	_____	_____
4. Women shouldn't earn a higher salary than their husbands.	_____	_____
5. Couples should have the same level of education.	_____	_____
6. It's easy to save money.	_____	_____
7. It's smart to use a credit card.	_____	_____
8. It's foolish to lend money to friends.	_____	_____

B. Take turns asking a partner about the statements above.

EXAMPLE:

A: Do you think it's difficult to write in English?

B: Yes, I do.

A: That's interesting. I don't. I like to write in English.

B: Do you think it's easy to do well in high school?

A: No, I don't.

B: Neither do I. High school is very hard.

2 LISTENING

A. 🎧 David and Danny are twins. How are they alike? How are they different? Listen to the interview and complete the chart.

Alike	Different	
They both . . .	*David . . .*	*Danny . . .*

B. Discuss with a partner: Do you know any twins? How are they alike and different?

3 INTERVIEW

Interview a partner. Use the questions below. Add more questions.

A: What subjects did you like in school/in high school/in university?

B: I liked _____ and _____ .

A: Why did you like _____ ?

B: Because _____ .

A: Do you think it's important to study _____ ?

B: _____ .

A: Which subjects didn't you like?

B: _____ .

A: Why not?

B: _____ .

A: Did you have to study _____ ?

B: _____ .

A: _____ ?

4 GAME

Play the game with a partner.

A. Write your name on a small piece of paper.

B. Move your paper by flipping a coin.

 = one space   = two spaces

C. Answer the question or do the task on the space.

Start	**1.** What are two kinds of math courses?	**2.** Use "hit it off" in a sentence.	**3.** Correct the sentence: I like to shop, and neither does my best friend.
7. What are two kinds of art courses?	**6.** What does "shop until you drop" mean?	**5.** Complete the sentence: I don't think it is important for couples to have the same _____ .	**4.** Which one doesn't belong? chemistry, physics, algebra, biology
8. Unscramble and answer: lend/is/it/to/money/to/foolish/family members/?	**9.** Complete the sentence: I usually _____ , and so does _____ .	**10.** What courses do high school students have to take?	**11.** Unscramble and agree or disagree: students/my/wear/opinion/uniforms/in/shouldn't.
Finish	**14.** Complete the sentence: I don't like _____ , and neither does _____ .	**13.** Unscramble and answer: should/credit cards/have/teenagers/?	**12.** Use "swamped" in a sentence.

1 VOCABULARY: *Travel preferences*

A. YOU FIRST. *Would you rather* _____ *or* _____ *?* Check (✓) your answers.

1. ☐ **travel alone**   ☐ **travel with someone**   2. ☐ **travel light**   ☐ **travel with everything you might need**

3. ☐ **rough it**   ☐ **stay in a nice hotel**   4. ☐ **plan your own trip**   ☐ **take a tour**

B. 🎧 PRONUNCIATION. Listen and practice the questions above.

C. PAIR UP and TALK. Ask your partner about travel. How are you the same? How are you different? Fill in the chart.

> Would you rather travel alone or travel with someone?

> I'd rather travel alone.

I would rather . . .	Both of us would rather . . .	My partner would rather . . .

D. REPORT. Tell your classmates about one similarity between you and your partner.

A. 🎧 **FIRST LISTENING.** Where has each person visited? Check (✓) the countries.

	Australia	Brazil	Canada	Chile	China	England	Japan	Korea	Morocco
1. Marco									
2. Minhee									
3. Ana									

B. 🎧 **SECOND LISTENING.** Match the people with what they did and what they said.

	What did the person do?	What did the person say?
1. Marco	took the wrong train	"It was very uncomfortable."
2. Minhee	rode a camel	"There wasn't anything I could do, so I just relaxed."
3. Ana	skated to university	"It beats the traffic in São Paulo."

IDIOM

It beats . . . =
It's better than . . .

C. PAIR UP and TALK. What was your most interesting travel experience?

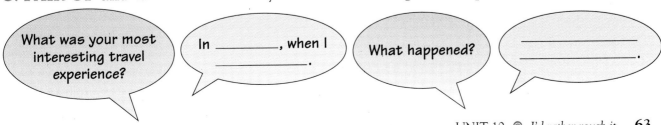

What was your most interesting travel experience?

In _____, when I _____.

What happened?

_____ _____.

A. 🎧 **PRONUNCIATION.** Listen and practice the questions and answers.

PRESENT PERFECT	
Have you ever **been** abroad?	Yes, I **have**.
Have you ever **flown** in an airplane?	Yes, I **have**.
Have you ever **taken** a tour?	No, I **haven't**.

PAST TENSE
I **went** to Italy when I was ten.
I **flew** to Hong Kong last year.

PAST PARTICIPLES

Irregular*				Regular	
be	been	take	taken	travel	traveled
eat	eaten	see	seen	talk	talked
fly	flown	lose	lost	climb	climbed
go	gone	leave	left	stay	stayed
*See page 100 for more irregular verbs.				rent	rented

More Pronunciation Practice:
Review of "-ed" endings
Turn to page 89.

B. GET IT RIGHT. Complete the questions and answers. Then ask a partner the questions. Give true answers.

1. A: Have you ever _____ to Italy? (be)

   B: Yes, I _____ . I _____ in Italy last summer.

2. A: Have you ever _____ in an airplane? (fly)

   B: No, I _____ .

3. A: Have you ever _____ on a camping trip? (go)

   B: No, I _____ .

4. A: Have you ever _____ something on a trip? (lose)

   B: Yes, I _____ . One time I _____ my wallet.

5. A: Have you ever _____ a mountain? (climb)

   B: Yes, I _____ . I _____ Mt. Fuji last year.

C. YOUR TURN. Ask a partner three more questions about traveling. You can use the ideas in the box or your own ideas. Remember to expand your answers.

Have you ever seen a wild animal?

Yes, I have. I saw a bear in Alaska.

stay in a luxury hotel	rent a car
go on a cruise	travel alone
take a ferry	travel abroad

4 CONVERSATION STRATEGY: *Asking follow-up questions*

A. 🎧 **PRONUNCIATION.** Listen and practice the questions.

> What did you visit?

> Did you have a good time?

> Was it fun?

> Where did you stay?

B. 🎧 **LISTEN and ADD.** Write the missing questions. Then practice with a partner.

1. A: Have you ever been to Mexico City?

B: Yes, I have. I went there last year.

A: _____

B: At a small hotel.

2. A: Have you ever taken a tour?

B: Yes, I have. I took a tour to London.

A: _____

B: It was fantastic!

5 TALKATHON: *Have you ever . . . ?*

A. TALK AROUND. Find classmates who have done these things. Then ask questions to get more information.

> Have you ever met someone famous?

> Yes, I have.

> Who did you meet?

Find someone who has . . .	Name	More information
1. met someone famous.		
2. been on TV.		
3. lost something valuable.		
4. done something dangerous.		
5. taken an unusual tour.		
6. stayed up all night.		

B. REPORT. Who had the most interesting experience?

Travel Laughs

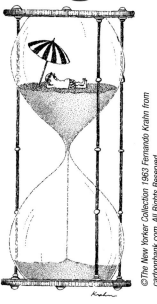

Travel Quotes

"I love to travel, but hate to arrive." —ALBERT EINSTEIN

"The world is a book, and those who do not travel read only a page." —ST. AUGUSTINE

"For my part, I travel not to go anywhere, but to go. I travel for travel's sake. . . ." —ROBERT LOUIS STEVENSON

"Trips do not end when you return home— usually this is the time when they really begin." —AGNES E. BENEDICT

Topic of the Day

What type of traveler are you?

1. The Lifetime Traveler

Lifetime travelers live to travel. When they aren't traveling, they are thinking about the next place to go. They enjoy both the good and the bad times.

2. The Adventurer

For adventurers, it isn't enough just to be in a new place. Adventurers need to do something new and different. They love travel only when it includes adventure. Adventures can be anything from bungee jumping to ostrich riding.

3. The Comfort Traveler

The comfort traveler is almost the opposite of the adventurer. The comfort traveler loves to travel only when it is easy and comfortable. Comfort travelers are especially happy on warm, sunny beaches. They don't need to do anything or go anywhere. One thing that's important to comfort travelers is the view from their room.

4. The Athlete Traveler

Athlete travelers like to plan vacations around sports. They go on golfing, tennis, mountain-climbing, or scuba-diving vacations. They may love to sit on a beach but only after spending an afternoon sailing or kayaking.

5. The Student Traveler

Student travelers love to learn about other places, languages, and cultures. They enjoy visiting museums and historical sites.

READ ABOUT IT

A. Answer the questions.

Travel Laughs
1. What does the sand in the hourglass represent?

Travel Quotes
2. Which writer thinks that everyone should travel?
3. Which writer thinks that travel has an impact *after* it is over?

Topic of the Day
4. Which type of traveler stays in expensive hotels?
5. Which type of traveler probably enjoys the journey as much as the destination?

B. Compare answers with a partner.

TALK ABOUT IT

Discuss the questions with a partner.

Travel Laughs
1. Do you usually feel tired or rested after a vacation?

Travel Quotes
2. Which two writers could probably travel well together?

Topic of the Day
3. Which types of travelers could travel happily together and which could not?
4. Which type of traveler are you? Do any of your friends or family fit these categories?

WRITE ABOUT IT

A. Make up a traveler type. Make notes.

The name of this traveler type: _____

A description of this traveler type: _____

What this traveler likes to do: _____

B. Write about your traveler type.

EXAMPLE:

> ### The Complainer
> Some people travel just to feel better about home. They complain about everything from their hotel rooms to the weather. Nothing is ever good enough for them. These travelers travel because they love the way they feel when they get back home.

> **Project Idea**
> **Travel Itinerary:**
> **The Perfect Vacation**
> Choose a traveler type. Design the perfect vacation for this traveler. Create an itinerary and illustrate it.

11 Are you stressed out?

1 VOCABULARY: *Signs of stress*

A. YOU FIRST. *How often do you* _____*?* Write *pretty often, sometimes, hardly ever,* or *never* in the blanks.

1. feel stressed out

_____

2. feel angry

_____

3. get an upset stomach

_____

4. have trouble sleeping

_____

5. get headaches

_____

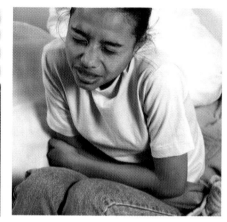

6. have trouble concentrating

_____

B. 🎧 PRONUNCIATION. Listen and practice the questions above.

C. PAIR UP and TALK. Ask a partner the questions.

> How often do you feel stressed out?

> I hardly ever feel stressed out.

> Really? You're lucky.

D. REPORT. Tell your classmates one thing about your partner.

A. LOOK/THINK/GUESS. What's happening? What is Ben doing?

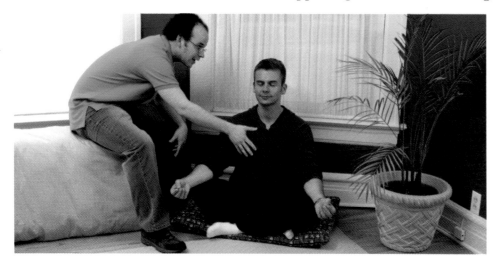

B. 🎧 **MODEL CONVERSATION.** Listen and practice.

Zack: Hey, Ben. What's up? Hello, Ben? Can you hear me?

Ben: Huh? What?

Zack: What are you doing?

Ben: I'm meditating . . .

Zack: Meditating? Why?

Ben: I'm stressed out, so Lucy told me to meditate.

Zack: Oh, I see. Why don't you just get some exercise?

Ben: Exercise?

Zack: Yeah. When I'm stressed out, I go for a run.

Ben: I don't know. . . . Maybe it's better to take it easy . . .

> **IDIOM**
>
> **take it easy** = relax

C. 🎧 **ACTIVE LISTENING.** Listen to the rest of the conversation. What else does Ben do? Check (✓) the things he does.

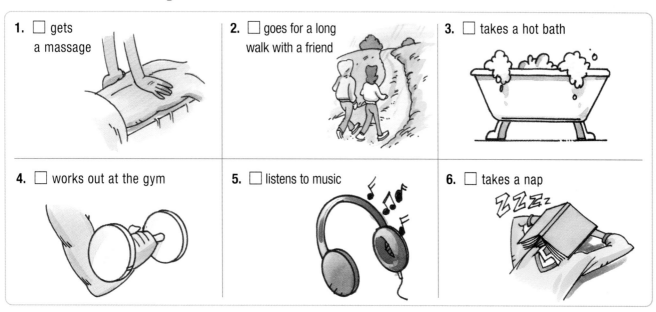

1. ☐ gets a massage

2. ☐ goes for a long walk with a friend

3. ☐ takes a hot bath

4. ☐ works out at the gym

5. ☐ listens to music

6. ☐ takes a nap

A. 🎧 PRONUNCIATION. Listen and practice the questions and answers.

QUESTIONS	ANSWERS
What do you do **when you feel stressed out**? **When you feel stressed out,** what do you do?	**(When I feel stressed out,)** I watch a movie. I watch a movie **(when I feel stressed out)**.
What do you do **when you feel nervous**? **When you feel nervous,** what do you do?	I talk to my friends **(when I feel nervous)**. **(When I feel nervous,)** I talk to my friends.

More Pronunciation Practice:

Reduced form of "wh-" questions with "do" Turn to page 90.

22

B. GET IT RIGHT. Complete the sentences in column A with the ideas from column B. Many different sentences are possible. Then compare sentences with a partner.

A	B
1. When I'm hungry in the afternoon, _____	**a.** I try to relax.
2. When someone makes me angry, _____	**b.** I drink some water.
3. When I feel sleepy in class, _____	**c.** I don't answer the phone.
4. When I have to give a speech, _____	**d.** I drink coffee.
5. When I'm tired during the day, _____	**e.** I try to ignore it.
6. When I have a cold, _____	**f.** I eat a snack.
7. When I don't have any money, _____	**g.** I get nervous.
8. When someone calls me late at night, _____	**h.** I get a headache.
	i. I try to get some rest.

C. YOUR TURN. Write three questions. Then ask a partner the questions.

1. What do you do when _____?

2. What do you do when _____?

3. When _____, what do you do?

> *What do you do when you have a headache?*

> *I take an aspirin, or I try to get some rest.*

4 CONVERSATION STRATEGY: *Making a polite request*

A. 🎧 **PRONUNCIATION.** Listen and practice the questions.

May I ask you a question?

Excuse me. Could I ask you a question?

B. 🎧 **LISTEN and ADD.** Write the missing questions. Then practice with a partner.

1. A: _____

B: Sure.

A: When do you get stressed out?

B: When I have too much work or when I'm worried about money.

2. A: _____

B: Go right ahead.

A: When do you get stressed out?

B: When I have family problems or when I have to study for an exam.

5 TALKATHON: *All about stress*

A. TALK AROUND. Ask six classmates the questions in the survey.

Name	Causes *When do you get stressed out?*	Effects *What happens when you get stressed out?*	Remedies *How do you deal with stress?*
Franco	When I have too much work.	I can't sleep.	I take a hot bath before bed.
1.			
2.			
3.			
4.			
5.			
6.			

B. REPORT. Join two classmates. Look at your surveys and find the most common cause of, effect of, and remedy for stress. Tell your classmates.

Stress Laughs

". . . happy birthday dear Mother, happy birthday to you!"

Facts on File

1. Headaches, stomachaches, muscle soreness, trouble sleeping, difficulty concentrating, and getting angry easily are all signs of stress.
2. Students with *some stress* learn better than students with *a lot of stress* and students with *no stress* at all.
3. The loss of a job, divorce, moving to a new town or school, having a baby, and the death of a husband, wife, or child are the events that cause people the most stress.
4. White sugar and the caffeine in coffee cause the body to feel stress.
5. Stress is caused by how we think and react to situations, not by the situations themselves. In other words, different people in the same situation feel different amounts of stress.

Headline News

The Sun

Can Chocolate Cure Stress?

When you are stressed out or angry, do you ever want a bowl of ice cream or a piece of chocolate? If so, you are not alone. When people are under stress, they often have cravings for sweet foods such as ice cream, chocolate, or cake.

There may be a biological reason for these cravings. Scientists studied rats under stress. The rats chose to eat sweet, high-energy foods after experiencing stress for a long time. Eating these foods helped the rats calm down. So if you have to calm down very quickly, a piece of chocolate may be a good idea!

READ ABOUT IT

A. Answer the questions.

Stress Laughs
1. How do you think the mother feels?

Facts on File
2. What events cause the most stress?
3. Which fact means "Some stress is better than none"?

Headline News
4. How do scientists know that eating sweet foods can help stress?
5. What are some examples of foods that help stress?

B. Compare answers with a partner.

TALK ABOUT IT

Discuss the questions with a partner.

Stress Laughs
1. What do you think the mother is going to do next? Why?
2. What is a good way to deal with stress in a situation like this one?

Facts on File
3. Fact #1 lists some signs of stress. Can you think of some other signs of stress?

Headline News
4. Do you ever eat sweet foods when you feel stressed or angry? If so, how do they make you feel?
5. What do you think is the best way to deal with stress? Why?

WRITE ABOUT IT

A. Think about a time when you felt very stressed out. Make notes.

The situation: _____

Your reaction or feelings: _____

How or why those feelings went away: _____

B. Write about your experiences.

EXAMPLE:

Last week everything went wrong. First my car broke down on the way to work. Then I spilled coffee on my clothes. Finally, my computer crashed and I lost a lot of my work. At first I stayed calm and relaxed, but by the time my computer crashed, I couldn't take it anymore. I started to cry, and then I felt better.

Project Idea
Advertisement: A Cure for Stress
Create a new cure for stress. Design an advertisement for it. Display the advertisements and have a gallery walk to look at them.

12 I've never heard of her.

1 VOCABULARY: *Professions*

A. YOU FIRST. *Who are some* _____ *?* Write your answers.

1. famous scientists

_____

_____

2. talented athletes

_____

_____

3. popular writers

_____

_____

4. respected political leaders

_____

_____

5. wealthy businesspeople

_____

_____

6. successful artists

_____

_____

B. 🎧 PRONUNCIATION. Listen and practice the questions above.

C. PAIR UP and TALK. Ask and answer the questions. Together list as many names as you can.

> Who are some famous scientists?

> Well, there's _____.

> What is she famous for?

> She _____.

D. REPORT. For which profession did you think of the most names?

A. LOOK/THINK/GUESS. Why does Ben go to the other table?

B. 🎧 **MODEL CONVERSATION.** Listen and practice.

Zack: Did you see the TV show about Jane Austen last night?

Ben: Jane who?

Zack: Jane Austen. You know, the famous British writer.

Ben: I've never heard of her.

Zack: Sure you have. She wrote *Pride and Prejudice* and *Emma* and a lot of other books.

Ben: Has she written anything recently?

Zack: No, Ben. She died in 1817.

Ben: Oh. What did she write about?

Zack: Oh, you know. Family life, love, marriage . . .

Ben: Excuse me, Zack. There's Sophie. I want to ask her out. Can I talk to you later?

Zack: Sure, Ben.

> **IDIOM**
>
> **ask her out** = invite her to go on a date

C. 🎧 **ACTIVE LISTENING.** Read the questions below. Then listen to the rest of the conversation and circle *a*, *b*, or *c*.

1. What is Sophie going to do this weekend?
 a. stay home
 b. go to a concert
 c. work

2. What kind of book is Sophie reading?
 a. a history book
 b. a cookbook
 c. a novel

3. What does Ben think of the book?
 a. He hasn't read it.
 b. He loved it.
 c. He doesn't say.

4. What does Ben say about Jane Austen?
 a. Who is she?
 b. She's the best.
 c. She's well-dressed.

A. 🎧 PRONUNCIATION. Listen and practice the questions and answers.

PAST

What year **were** you **born**?	I **was born** in 1976.
Where **did** you **grow up**?	In San Francisco.
When **did** you **graduate** from high school?	I **graduated** from high school in 1994.
Who **was** your favorite teacher?	My algebra teacher.

PRESENT

Where **do** you **live**?	I **live** in New York.
What **do** you **do**?	I'm an engineer. I **work** for a large company.
How **do** you **spend** your free time?	I **listen** to music. I **work out** at the gym.

FUTURE

What **are** you **going to do** in the future?	I'm **going to get married**.
	I'm **going to start** my own company.

More Pronunciation Practice:

Intonation of "wh-" questions
Turn to page 91.

B. GET IT RIGHT. Unscramble the questions. Then ask a partner the questions.

1. were / where / born / you

_____ ?

2. you / born / were / when

_____ ?

3. did / where / you / elementary / school / go / to

_____ ?

4. you / now / live / where / do

_____ ?

5. spend / weekends / your / how / you / do

_____ ?

6. do / what / you / do

_____ ?

7. next / weekend / are / you / what / going / to / do

_____ ?

8. future / in / going / to / do / the / are / you / what

_____ ?

C. YOUR TURN. Write three more questions about the past, present, and future. Then ask a partner the questions.

4 CONVERSATION STRATEGY: *Saying you don't know*

A. 🎧 **PRONUNCIATION.** Listen and practice the expressions.

> I'm not really sure.

> Actually, I have no idea.

> I don't remember.

B. 🎧 **LISTEN and ADD.** Write the missing expressions. Then practice with a partner.

1. A: Who do you admire?

B: Pelé.

A: Who's Pelé?

B: He was the greatest soccer player of all time.

A: Oh. When did he start playing soccer?

B: _____ .

2. A: Who do you admire?

B: Midori. Have you heard of her?

A: No, I haven't.

B: She's a talented musician from Japan.

A: Oh. What's her full name?

B: _____ .

5 TWO-MINUTE INTERVIEWS: *Who do you admire?*

A. YOU FIRST. Choose a person you admire. It can be someone you know or someone famous. Answer the questions about the person in the diagram below.

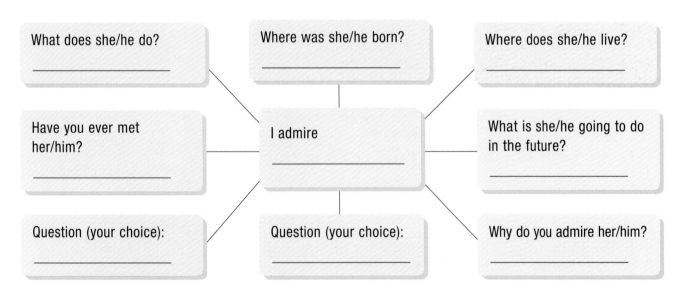

What does she/he do?
_____

Where was she/he born?
_____

Where does she/he live?
_____

Have you ever met her/him?
_____

I admire
_____

What is she/he going to do in the future?
_____

Question (your choice):
_____

Question (your choice):
_____

Why do you admire her/him?
_____

B. TALK AROUND. Interview a partner for two minutes about the person he or she admires. Then interview two more people.

C. REPORT. Tell an interesting fact about someone a classmate admires.

Fame Laughs

"Hello! What's this?"

In My Opinion

It is harder and harder to admire politicians these days. In fact, it is even difficult to trust politicians. That wasn't always true. In the eighteenth century, Benjamin Franklin was one of America's most famous politicians. Everyone trusted and admired him. He was sincere and honest. He was also extremely smart and creative. He was successful at everything he tried. Perhaps today's politicians should study the life of this great man or others like him.

Personal Opinions

We asked several people how they feel about being famous. Here's what they said:

"*Fame means everything to me. I love to be loved and to be known by many people. Fame is something great and nice.*"

— AMAL HIJAZI (Lebanese singer)

"*Fame is awful. You don't know who to trust. So many people want to be with you only because you are famous. It is very lonely being famous. It seems like everyone loves you, but you know that really no one loves you.*"

— A FAMOUS AMERICAN MOVIE STAR

"*I'm not interested in fame itself, but I am interested in what fame can do for my work. Once you are famous, everyone takes your work more seriously and your work finds its way into museums.*"

— YAYOI KUSAMA (Japanese artist)

READ ABOUT IT

A. Answer the questions.

Fame Laughs
1. What decision does this man need to make now?

In My Opinion
2. Who was Benjamin Franklin?
3. Why does the writer think politicians should study Benjamin Franklin's life?

Personal Opinions
4. Which of the personal thoughts on fame are positive and which are negative?

B. Compare answers with a partner.

TALK ABOUT IT

Discuss the questions with a partner.

Fame Laughs
1. Imagine you are this person. Which door would you choose? Explain why.

In My Opinion
2. Why did people admire Benjamin Franklin?
3. Make a list of four other admirable qualities.

Personal Opinions
4. Which two thoughts are opposites of each other, and which one do you think is more true?
5. Would you like to be famous? What would you like to be famous for?

WRITE ABOUT IT

A. What are your thoughts on fame? Make notes.

Is fame mostly positive or mostly negative? _____

What are the best and worst things about fame? _____

_____

B. Write about your thoughts on fame.

EXAMPLE:

> I think fame is terrible. When you are famous, everyone knows everything you do, especially all of the bad things. The newspapers like to say bad things about you. People like to think bad things about you, so everyone believes all the bad things they read in the newspaper. No one really knows the truth about famous people.

Project Idea
Collage:
What Is Fame?
Design a collage that shows the positive and negative sides of fame. Use pictures and words and phrases in English.

Review of Units 10–12

1 ROLE PLAYS

A. Work with a partner. Write a conversation for each picture.

1.

2.

B. Practice the conversations. Then perform your role plays for your classmates.

2 LISTENING

A. 🎧 Listen to the questions and write your answers.

1. _____
2. _____
3. _____
4. _____
5. _____
6. _____

B. 🎧 Listen again and write the questions. Then ask a partner the questions.

1. _____
2. _____
3. _____
4. _____
5. _____
6. _____

3 GAME: TWENTY QUESTIONS

Play the game in groups of four.

1. Take turns choosing a famous person.

2. The other students ask questions about the person. You can ask no more than twenty questions.

EXAMPLE:

Questions	Answers
Is the person a man or a woman?	A man.
Is he living or dead?	He's dead.
What was his profession?	He was an artist.
What was his nationality?	He was Italian.
What was he famous for?	He painted the *Mona Lisa*.
Is it Leonardo da Vinci?	Yes!

4 GAME

Divide into teams of three or four students. Two teams play together. Team A, look at the information below. Team B, turn to page 83.

Team A

1. Ask Team B the ten questions below. Team B gets one point for every correct answer.

2. Answer Team B's ten questions. You get one point for every correct answer.

3. The team with the most correct answers wins.

Travel preferences	Professions	Life history	Stress	Idioms
1. What does "I like to travel light" mean? 2. Where can you ice-skate to work or school in the winter?	3. Who are two businesspeople? 4. What are the names of a well-known female artist and a well-known male artist?	5. Where did Jane Austen live? 6. Where was our teacher born?	7. What are two signs of stress? 8. What are two popular ways to deal with stress?	9. Explain "It beats the traffic in Rio." 10. Use "ask him out" in a sentence.

STUDENT A

A. Read about Carlos and answer your partner's questions.

My name is Carlos Rivas. I live in Mexico, and I study English at the university. I'm going to work in tourism, so it's important for me to speak English. I try to use only English in class, but I sometimes speak Spanish. I don't worry about mistakes; I just speak up. We practice speaking with partners, and I usually ask follow-up questions. Now I want to improve my reading. I use the Internet every weekend, especially to find out about sports. Next summer I'm going to visit a friend in England.

B. Now ask your partner questions about Kanya.

1. Where does Kanya live? _____

2. Where does she study English? _____

3. What strategies does she use in class? _____

4. What strategies does she use outside of class? _____

5. What are her plans for the future? _____

6. In your opinion, is she a good language learner? _____

Review of Units 1–3, Activity 2: Information Gap for Student B

STUDENT B

A. Ask your partner questions about Carlos.

1. Where does Carlos live? _____

2. Where does he study English? _____

3. What strategies does Carlos use in class? _____

4. What strategies does he use outside of class? _____

5. What are his plans for the future? _____

6. In your opinion, is he a good language learner? _____

B. Read about Kanya and answer your partner's questions.

My name is Kanya Meesang, and I live in Thailand. I want to travel to Australia, so I study English at a language institute. I have a pen pal in Sydney, Australia. We send e-mails every week. I also listen to songs in English. In class I try to speak confidently and use new vocabulary words. I sometimes worry about making mistakes. I write new vocabulary words on flashcards and practice at home. I also use an English–English dictionary.

Review of Units 10–12, Activity 4: Information Gap for Student B

Team B

1. Answer Team A's ten questions. You get one point for every correct answer.

2. Ask Team A the ten questions below. Team A gets one point for every correct answer.

3. The team with the most correct answers wins.

Travel preferences	Professions	Life history	Stress	Idioms
1. Name one luxury hotel and one budget hotel in your area.	3. Who are two female political leaders?	5. Why is Pelé famous?	7. Does caffeine cause stress?	9. Explain "I don't like to rough it."
2. Where can you ride on a camel?	4. Who is a famous poet?	6. Where did our teacher grow up?	8. How does meditation help stress?	10. When do you say "Take it easy"?

More Pronunciation Practice

UNIT 1 Intonation of *yes/no* questions

A. 🎧 Listen and practice the questions. Notice the rising intonation.

Do you ever come to class late?

Do you usually look up new words?

Does your teacher always give you homework?

B. 🎧 Listen to the conversations. Then practice them with a partner.

1. A: Do you always do your homework?
B: Yes, I do.
A: Always?
B: Well, almost always.

2. A: Do you usually listen to the teacher?
B: Yes, I do. I always listen to the teacher.
A: Always?
B: Well, almost always.

3. A: Do you ever come to class late?
B: No, I don't.
A: Never?
B: Well, hardly ever.

4. A: Do you ever daydream in class?
B: No, I don't.
A: Never?
B: Well, hardly ever.

UNIT 2 Intonation of *wh-* questions

A. 🎧 Listen and practice the questions. Notice the rising and falling intonation.

When is the news on?

How many programs do you watch regularly?

Why are game shows popular?

B. 🎧 Listen to the chant. Then listen again and repeat it.

A: What's a good sitcom?
B: I don't know.
A: What channel is the weather on?
B: I don't know.
A: When's the news on?
B: I don't know.

A: What's a good talk show?
B: I don't know.
A: Why are game shows popular?
B: I don't know.
A: Why am I asking you?
B: Beats me.

C. Practice the chant with the whole class. Then practice it in two large groups.

UNIT 3 Reduced form of *going to*

A. 🎧 Listen and practice the questions. Notice two ways to say *going to*.

1. What are you going to do on Monday morning?

2. Are you going to study?

3. Where are you going to be on Monday night?

4. Are you going to be at home?

B. 🎧 Listen to the conversation. Then practice it with a partner.

A: Are you going to take a vacation this year?

B: Yes, definitely.

A: Where are you going to go?

B: To the beach.

A: How long are you going to stay?

B: About a week.

A: Who are you going to go with?

B: With my family.

A: Are you going to drive your car?

B: Probably.

A: It's going to be fun.

B: I hope so!

C. Ask your partner three questions with *going to*.

UNIT 4 Reduced form of *can*

A. 🎧 Listen and practice the questions and answers. Notice the difference in the way *can* is pronounced.

Reduced	Not reduced
Can I get there by bus? Can I get there by train? When can I call you? You can call me tomorrow.	No, you can't. You can't get there by bus. Yes, you can.

B. 🎧 Listen to the conversations. Then practice them with a partner.

1. A: Can I call you tomorrow?
   B: Yes, you can. You can call me in the morning.

2. A: When can we meet?
   B: We can meet on Wednesday.
   A: I can't meet on Wednesday. Can we meet on Thursday?
   B: Sure.

3. A: Where can I get the airport bus?
   B: You can get it at the city station.
   A: Can I buy a ticket on the bus?
   B: No, you can't. But you can buy it at the station.

4. A: Where can I check the weather forecast?
   B: You can check it online, or you can check the newspaper.

UNIT 5 Sentence stress

In sentences, content words (nouns and pronouns, verbs, adverbs, adjectives) are stressed. Function words (all the other words) are usually unstressed. The last content word usually gets the most stress.

A. 🎧 Listen and practice.

A **vet's job** is more **dangerous** than a **doctor's**.

Who has an **easier job**, a **teacher** of **children** or a **teacher** of **adults**?

B. 🎧 Listen and practice. Only stress the content words.

1. A **police officer's job** is **dangerous**.
   A **police officer's job** is **dangerous** and **difficult**.
   A **police officer's job** is more **dangerous** and **difficult** than a **vet's**.
   Is a **police officer's job** more **dangerous** and **difficult** than a **vet's**?

2. An **engineer gets** a **good salary**.
   Does an **engineer get** a **good salary**?
   Does an **engineer get** a **better salary** than a **firefighter**?

3. A **waiter has** an **easy job**.
   A **waiter has** an **easier job** than a **chef**.
   Does a **waiter have** an **easier job** than a **chef**?

4. An **architect gets** a **good salary**.
   Does an **architect get** a **good salary**?
   Does an **architect get** a **better salary** than a **lawyer**?

UNIT 6 Intonation of *or* questions

A. 🎧 Listen and practice the questions. Notice the rising intonation on the first part of the question and the falling intonation on the second part.

Are you messy or neat?

Who is older—your mother or your father?

B. 🎧 Listen and practice the questions.

1. Do you prefer jazz or rock music?
2. Do you prefer to drink coffee or tea?
3. Do you like to study at home or at school?

4. Are you a morning person or a night person?
5. Would you rather go to a reggae concert or a basketball game?
6. Would you rather watch soccer or play soccer?

C. Ask a partner the questions in B.

UNIT 7 Syllable stress in two-syllable words

Most two-syllable words in English have a stressed syllable and an unstressed syllable. The vowel in the unstressed syllable is usually pronounced "uh" or "ih." This sound is called a schwa (ə).

Stress on the first syllable		Stress on the second syllable
language	student	prefer
Russian	schedule	forgot
English	listen	exam
science	welcome	commute

A. 🎧 Listen to the words. Notice that the vowels in the unstressed syllables have a similar sound.

B. 🎧 Listen and practice.

1. Parents and children are welcome.
2. Did you take Russian as a foreign language?
3. Do the students have a long commute?

4. I forgot to check my schedule.
5. Do you prefer to listen to Spanish or English?
6. She forgot to study for her science exam.

UNIT 8 Embedded questions

A. 🎧 Listen and practice the questions.

Do you think it's easy to spend money?   Do you think it's important to pay bills?

B. 🎧 Listen and practice.

1. pay bills
to pay bills
important to pay bills
think it's important to pay bills
Do you think it's important to pay bills?

2. lend it
borrow money or lend it
better to borrow money or lend it
it's better to borrow money or lend it
think it's better to borrow money or lend it
Do you think it's better to borrow money or
       lend it?

3. save money
to save money
easy to save money
it's easy to save money
think it's easy to save money
Do you think it's easy to save money?

4. part-time job
have a part-time job
good to have a part-time job
think it's good to have a part-time job
Do you think it's good to have a part-time job?

5. wear uniforms
should wear uniforms
students should wear uniforms
high school students should wear uniforms
think high school students should wear
       uniforms
Do you think high school students should wear
       uniforms?

UNIT 9 Reduced form of *does he, does she*

A. 🎧 Listen and practice the questions and statements. Notice two ways to say *does he* and *does she*.

Does he like horror movies?   Does he play golf?

Does she like horror movies?   Does she play golf?

I like horror movies, and so does he.   She doesn't play golf, and neither does he.

I like horror movies, and so does she.   He doesn't like golf, and neither does she.

B. 🎧 Listen to the conversations. Then practice them with a partner.

1. A: Does he like to travel?
   B: No. He doesn't like to travel, and neither
      does she.

2. A: Does he like action movies?
   B: Yes, he does.
   A: So you like action movies, and so does he.
   B: That's right.

3. A: Does she want to play tennis?
   B: No. She doesn't want to play tennis, and
      neither does he.

4. A: Does she work there?
   B: Yes, she does.
   A: So you work there, and so does she.
   B: You got it.

UNIT 10 Review of -ed endings

A. 🎧 Listen to the examples. Then listen again and practice them.

| talked | traveled | skated |

B. Work with a partner. Take turns reading the words. Do you hear /t/, /d/, or /ed/? Check (✓).

	/t/	/d/	/ed/
1. organized			
2. wanted			
3. called			
4. asked			
5. looked			
6. decided			
7. loved			
8. hated			
9. wanted			
10. liked			
11. watched			
12. planned			

C. 🎧 Listen to the words above. Were your answers correct?

D. 🎧 Listen to the conversation. Then practice it with a partner.

A: How was your vacation?

B: Well, I loved it, but my friends hated it.

A: Really? Why's that?

B: Well, I organized it. I wanted to rent a house by the beach, so I called the travel agency and asked about houses. I looked at two places and decided to rent a house right on the beach.

A: I see.

B: It was very noisy. My friends wanted privacy, but I liked it. I watched the people on the beach. My friends watched television. We planned to stay for two weeks, but we only stayed one week.

A. 🎧 Listen to the questions. Notice two ways to say *what do you*.

What do you do when you have a cold?

When you have a cold, what do you do?

What do you do when you don't have any money?

When you don't have any money, what do you do?

B. 🎧 Listen to the chant. Then listen again and repeat it.

A: What do you do when you're angry?

B: What do you do when you're mad?

A: What do you do when you're lonely?

B: What do you do when you're sad?

A: What do you do when it's raining?

B: What do you do when it's gray?

A: What do you do when it's windy?

B: What do you do on a really cold day?

A: Where do you go when it's sunny?

B: Where do you go when it's hot?

A: Where do you go when you have money?

B: Where do you go when you do not?

C. Practice the chant with the whole class. Then practice it in two large groups.

D. Ask a partner four of the questions in the chant.

A. 🎧 Listen to the questions and responses. Notice the rising intonation in the responses.

A: What year were you born?

B: What year was I born?

A: Where do you live?

B: Where do I live?

B. 🎧 Listen to the conversations. Then practice them with a partner.

1. A: Where were you born?
B: Where was I born?
A: Yes.
B: I was born in Boston.

2. A: Where did you grow up?
B: Where did I grow up?
A: Uh-huh.
B: I grew up in Boston.

3. A: When did you graduate from high school?
B: When did I graduate from high school?
A: Yes.
B: I'm still in high school.

4. A: What do you do on weekends?
B: What do I do on weekends? Not much.

5. A: What are you going to do next weekend?
B: What am I going to do next weekend?
A: Yes.
B: I'm not sure.

C. Practice the conversations again. Use your own answers.

Conversation Strategies Summary

UNIT 1 Confirming what you heard

Do you have the homework assignment from Friday's class? →
- Friday's class?
- Did you say Friday's class?

UNIT 2 Pausing

How many hours of TV do you usually watch every day? →
- Hmmm. Well, I guess . . .
- I don't know. Let me see . . .
- Let me think . . .

UNIT 3 Keeping the conversation going

I'm going to go to Hawaii for vacation. →
- Who are you going to go with?
- Where are you going to stay?
- How are you going to get there?

UNIT 4 Asking for recommendations

- Can you recommend a good website?
- What's a good website? →

There's a good website called International Penpals dot com.

UNIT 5 Expanding your answer

Would you rather be a boss or an employee? →

I'd rather be a boss. The salary is higher, and the work is more interesting.

UNIT 6 Showing you are interested

My sister is the funniest person in my family. →
- Really?
- Is that so?
- Oh, yeah?
- I see.

UNIT 7 Expressing opinions

- In my opinion, high school students should work part time.
- I think high school students should wear uniforms.
- I feel strongly that students should study every night.
- I don't think parents should help children with their homework.

UNIT 8 Reaching a compromise

I think we should stay at the Palm Inn.

- I like that idea because the Palm Inn is near the beach.
- That makes sense to me.
- Why don't we stay at a cheaper hotel?
- I'd rather stay at a nicer hotel.

UNIT 9 Ending a conversation

Well, I have to go.

- Nice talking to you.
- Good talking to you.

UNIT 10 Asking follow-up questions

I went to London last year.

- What did you visit?
- Did you have a good time?
- Was it fun?
- Where did you stay?

UNIT 11 Making a polite request

- May I ask you a question?
- Excuse me. Could I ask you a question?

Sure.

UNIT 12 Saying you don't know

When was he born?

- I'm not really sure.
- Actually, I have no idea.
- I don't remember.

Vocabulary Summary

Nouns

assignment	learner
class	questions
friends	teacher
gum	vocabulary
homework	words

Verbs

ask	guess
chew	listen
come	look up
daydream	sit
doodle	speak
fall asleep	use
forget	write down

Frequency adverbs

almost always	never
always	sometimes
ever	usually
hardly ever	

Prepositions

in
next to
outside of

Time expression

in the morning

Expressions

Just a minute.
Not again!
What's up?

Other new words I learned

_____

_____

_____

_____

_____

_____

Nouns: *Kinds of TV shows*

game show
sitcom (situation comedy)
soap opera
sports
talk show
the news

Other nouns

channel	show
hour	station

Adjectives

average	popular
favorite	typical
funny	

Verbs

dislike	watch
like	

Time expression

almost every day

Question words

how many	when
what	why

Expressions

Are you there?
What's happening?
Not much.

Other new words I learned

_____

_____

_____

_____

_____

_____

UNIT 3

Nouns
beach
bike tour
CD
concert
day trip
family
friends
home
honeymoon

Adjectives
athletic
dangerous
exciting
fun
interesting
romantic
unusual

Verbs
be going to
buy
do
drive
go sightseeing
go surfing
hang out
stay
take
visit
want to

Time expressions
next week
on your next vacation
this weekend

Question words
how
how long
where
who

Expression
out of town

Other new words I learned

_____ _____ _____
_____ _____ _____

UNIT 4

Nouns
bus station
cell phone
e-mail address
Internet café
movie listings
newspaper
online
phone number
schedule
sports score
ticket
voice mail
weather forecast
website

Verbs
call
can
check
contact
find
look
return

Expressions
Could you give me a ring?
Please leave a message.
Talk to you soon.

Other new words I learned

_____ _____ _____
_____ _____ _____

UNIT 5

Nouns: *Jobs*
accountant
architect
bookstore owner
chef
computer programmer
doctor
engineer
firefighter
flight attendant
lawyer
police officer
travel agent
vet

Other nouns
boss
commute
job security
salary
work

Adjectives
better
crazy
easy
famous
good
good-looking
happy
high
long
old
rich
smart
stressful
worse
young

Expression
It's a breeze.

Other new words I learned

UNIT 6

Nouns
career
hobbies
middle child
only child
personal characteristics
personalities
siblings
uncle

Adjectives
best
hardworking
lazy
messy
neat
outgoing
quiet
relaxed
serious
worst

Expression
She's a riot.

Other new words I learned

Unit 7

Nouns: School subjects
algebra
art
biology
calculus
chemistry
film history
foreign language
history
literature
math
painting
science
sculpture

Other nouns
course
high school
subject
uniform
university

Adjectives
British
European
Russian
part-time
practical
useful

Verbs
feel
think
wear
work

Modals
have to/don't have to
should/shouldn't

Expression
I'm pretty swamped.

Other new words I learned

_____
_____

_____
_____

_____
_____

Unit 8

Nouns
bank
cash
charity
clothes
credit card
department store
dolphin
gift
helicopter
motorbike
nightclub
ride
saver
spender

Adjectives
broke
foolish
hard

Verbs
borrow
carry
give
go sailing
lend
put
rent
save
spend
swim

Expressions
I love to shop until I drop.
It's easy come, easy go.

Other new words I learned

_____
_____

_____
_____

_____
_____

Unit 9

Nouns
amount
blood type
couple
interests
level of education
religion
taste in movies
tennis

Adjectives
alike
bored
different
talkative
tired

Adverbs
neither
so

Verbs
go on a date with
go out
hit it off

Expressions
Oh, it was okay, I guess.
You have a lot in common.
You're just too much alike.

Other new words I learned

_____
_____

_____
_____

_____
_____

Unit 10

Nouns
airplane
animal
camel
camping trip
car
cruise
ferry
hotel
mountain
tour
trip
wallet

Pronouns
everything
someone

Adjectives
alone
fancy
light
luxury
wrong

Verbs
climb
fly
lose
meet
plan
ride
rough it
see
skate
stay up all night
travel

Expressions
I just relaxed.
It beats the traffic in . . .

Other new words I learned

_____
_____

_____
_____

_____
_____

UNIT 11

Nouns
aspirin
backache
bath
cause
cold
effect
exercise
headache
massage
remedy
rest
snack
speech
stomach

Adjectives
angry
nervous
sleepy
stressed out
upset
worried

Verbs
deal with
have trouble _____ing
ignore
meditate
take a nap
work out

Expressions
Take it easy.
Go right ahead.

Other new words I learned

_____   _____   _____

_____   _____   _____

UNIT 12

Nouns
artist
athlete
businessperson
fame
musician
political leader
profession
scientist
soccer player
writer

Adjectives
famous
popular
respected
successful
talented
wealthy
well-known

Verbs
admire
ask (her) out
be born
graduate
grow up

Expressions
_____ who?
Sure you have.

Other new words I learned

_____   _____   _____

_____   _____   _____

Irregular Verbs

Present	Simple Past	Past Participle	Present	Simple Past	Past Participle
be	was/were	been	lend	lent	lent
become	became	become	lose	lost	lost
begin	began	begun	make	made	made
break	broke	broken	meet	met	met
bring	brought	brought	pay	paid	paid
buy	bought	bought	put	put	put
catch	caught	caught	read	read	read
choose	chose	chosen	ride	rode	ridden
come	came	come	run	ran	run
cost	cost	cost	say	said	said
do	did	done	see	saw	seen
draw	drew	drawn	sell	sold	sold
drink	drank	drunk	send	sent	sent
drive	drove	driven	shut	shut	shut
eat	ate	eaten	sing	sang	sung
fall	fell	fallen	sleep	slept	slept
feel	felt	felt	speak	spoke	spoken
fight	fought	fought	spend	spent	spent
find	found	found	stand	stood	stood
fly	flew	flown	steal	stole	stolen
forget	forgot	forgotten	swim	swam	swum
get	got	gotten	take	took	taken
give	gave	given	teach	taught	taught
go	went	gone	tell	told	told
grow	grew	grown	think	thought	thought
have	had	had	throw	threw	thrown
hear	heard	heard	understand	understood	understood
hit	hit	hit	wake	woke	woken
keep	kept	kept	wear	wore	worn
know	knew	known	win	won	won
leave	left	left	write	wrote	written

Credits

ILLUSTRATIONS

Reggie Holladay 21, 51, 69
Jonathan Massie 21, 61
Bill Petersen 22

PHOTOGRAPHICS CREDITS

2 *(top, left to right)* © Jack Demuth; © Christina Kennedy/PhotoEdit; © Colin Young-Wolff/PhotoEdit; *(bottom, left to right)* © Christina Kennedy/PhotoEdit; © Stockbyte /SuperStock; © Royalty-Free/CORBIS

3 *(both)* © Jack Demuth. Special thanks to Oakton Community College, Des Plaines, Illinois

5 © Digital Vision/PictureQuest

6 *(top)* © Digital Vision/PictureQuest; *(bottom)* © Jack Demuth

8 *(top, left to right)* Photofest; © David Young-Wolff/PhotoEdit; Photofest; *(bottom, all)* © David Young-Wolff/PhotoEdit

9 *(both)* © Jack Demuth

10 © Douglas Kirkland/CORBIS

11 © Justin Pumfrey/Getty Images

12 *(left)* © Brad Loper/Dallas Morning News/CORBIS ; *(right)* © The New Yorker Collection 1990 Peter Steiner from cartoonbank.com. All Rights Reserved

14 *(top, left to right)* © Chuck Savage/CORBIS; © Tony Anderson/PhotoDisc/Getty Images; eStock Photo/Reporters Press Agency/PictureQuest; *(bottom, left to right)* © Joe McBride/Getty Images; © Jeff Maloney/PhotoDisc/Getty Images; David Hanover/Getty Images

15 *(top, left to right)* © Myrleen Cate/PhotoEdit; © David Young-Wolff/PhotoEdit; © Larry Dale Gordon/Getty Images; *(bottom, left to right)* © Harald Sund/Getty Images; © R. Ian Lloyd/Masterfile; © Tim Mosenfelder/Getty Images

17 © Ed Kashi/CORBIS

18 *(top)* © David Young-Wolff/PhotoEdit; *(middle, left to right)* © Getty Images; © Stephen Frink/IndexStock Imagery/PictureQuest; *(bottom)* © The New Yorker Collection 1990 James Stevenson from cartoonbank.com. All Rights Reserved.

20 © Tim Pannell/CORBIS

23 *(left to right)* © Steve Cole/PhotoDisc/Getty Images;

© Digital Vision/Getty Images

24 © Jack Hollingsworth/PhotoDisc/Getty Images

25 © Sylvaine Achernar/Getty Images

26 *(top)* © The New Yorker Collection 2002 Mick Stevens from cartoonbank.com. All Rights Reserved; *(bottom)* Courtesy of IDEO

28 *(top, left to right)* © Royalty-Free/CORBIS; © Walter Hodges/Getty Images; © Mark Lewis/Getty Images; *(bottom, left to right)* © Mark Andersen/Rubberball Productions/Getty Images; © Fisher-Thatcher/Getty Images; © Stephen Simpson/Getty Images

29 *(top, left to right)* © Stewart Cohen/IndexStock; © Photodisc Collection/PhotoDisc/Getty Images; © Davide Wells/The Image Works; *(bottom, left to right)* © Royalty-Free/CORBIS; © Stephen Derr/Getty Images; © FK Photo/CORBIS

30 © Christopher Fitzgerald/The Image Works

32 *(top, left to right)* © The New Yorker Collection 2002 Barbara Smaller from cartoonbank.com. All Rights Reserved; © LWA-Dann Tardif/CORBIS; *(bottom)* © Eugene Gebhardt/Getty Images

34 *(top, left to right)* © Bob Daemmrich/The Image Works; © Ghislain & Marie David de Lossy/Getty Images; © Ronnie Kaufman/CORBIS; © Richard Hutchings/CORBIS; *(bottom, left to right)* © Darren Modricker/CORBIS; © Michael Newman/PhotoEdit; © Rob Lewine/CORBIS; © Kwame Zikomo/SuperStock

35 *(left to right)* © Rob Lewine/CORBIS; © Skjold/The Image Works; © SuperStock

36 © Tom & Dee Ann McCarthy/CORBIS

38 *(top)* © Larry Williams/CORBIS; *(bottom)* © The New Yorker Collection 2000 Barbara Smaller from cartoonbank.com. All Rights Reserved

40 *(top)* © Jeremy Maude/Masterfile; © Oscar C. Williams; *(bottom)* © John Springer Collection/CORBIS

41 © Brian Bailey/ImageState

42 *(top, left to right)* © Royalty-Free/CORBIS; © Nathan Benn/CORBIS; © Spencer Grant/PhotoEdit; *(bottom, left to right)* © Stewart Cohen/Getty Images; © Sean Justice/Getty Images; © Stewart Cohen/IndexStock

43 *(left to right)* © Paul Viant /Getty Images; © Jack Demuth

44 © Paul Viant/Getty Images

46 *(top)* © The New Yorker Collection 1986 Warren Miller from cartoonbank.com. All Rights Reserved; *(bottom)* © David Stoecklein/CORBIS

48 *(top, left to right)* © Brooklyn Production/CORBIS; © Royalty-Free/CORBIS; © Darren Modricker/CORBIS;

Credits (Continued)

(bottom, left to right) © Royalty-Free/CORBIS; © Jose Luis Pelaez/CORBIS; © Syracuse Newspapers/Al Campanie/The Image Works

49 (left to right) © Lonnie Duka/IndexStock; © Stuart Hughes/CORBIS; © Darryl Estrine/Getty Images; © ThinkStock LLC/IndexStock

50 © Petrified Collection/Getty Images

52 (top) © The New Yorker Collection 1992 Bernard Schoenbaum from cartoonbank.com. All Rights Reserved; (bottom) © Stephen Stickler/Getty Images

54 (top, left to right) © Michael Segal/SuperStock; © Royalty-Free/CORBIS; © ThinkStock/SuperStock; (bottom, left to right) © SuperStock; © Tony Freeman/PhotoEdit; © Arvind Garg/CORBIS

55 © Donna Day/Getty Images

56 © Rob Gage/Getty Images

57 © Nicolas Russell/Getty Images

58 (top) © Freitag/Zefa/Masterfile; (bottom) © The New Yorker Collection 1998 Sam Gross from cartoonbank.com. All Rights Reserved.

60 © K. Solveig/Zefa/Masterfile

61 © Royalty-Free/CORBIS

62 (top, left to right) © Jeff Greenberg/PhotoEdit; © Masterfile Royalty-Free/Masterfile; © Spencer Grant/PhotoEdit; © Masterfile Royalty-Free/Masterfile; (bottom, left to right) © Jeff Greenberg/The Image Works; © Larry Dale Gordon/Getty Images; © David Young-Wolff/PhotoEdit; © Thomas Hoeffgen/Getty Images

63 (left, top to bottom) © Rick Gomez/Masterfile; © Michael Newman/PhotoEdit; © Bob Daemmrich/The Image Works; (right, top to bottom) © Orion Press/Getty Images; © Lee Frost/Robert Harding/Getty Images; © Carl & Ann Purcell/CORBIS

64 © David Trood Pictures/Getty Images

66 (top) © The New Yorker Collection 1963 Fernando Krahn from cartoonbank.com. All Rights Reserved; (bottom) © T. Allofs/Zefa/Masterfile

68 (top, left to right) © Digital Vision/Getty Images; © Jeff Greenberg/PhotoEdit; © Mary Kate Denny/PhotoEdit; (bottom, left to right) © Rob Bartee/SuperStock; © G K & Vikki Hart/Getty Images; © Harriet Gans/The Image Works

69 © Jack Demuth

70 © Chip Simons/Getty Images

71 © Royalty-Free/CORBIS

72 (top) © The New Yorker Collection 1998 Jerry Marcus from cartoonbank.com. All Rights Reserved; (bottom) © BananaStock/SuperStock

74 (top, left to right) © Bettmann/CORBIS; © Pornchai Kittiwongsakul/AFP/Getty Images; © Reuters/CORBIS; (bottom, left to right) © PA/Topham/The Image Works; © Bill Pierce/Time Life Pictures/Getty Images; © Bettmann/CORBIS

75 (both) © Jack Demuth

76 © Tim MacPherson/Getty Images

78 (top, left to right) © The New Yorker Collection 1967 Henry Martin from cartoonbank.com. All Rights Reserved; © Stapleton Collection/CORBIS; (bottom) © Nogues Alain/CORBIS SYGMA

80 (left to right) © Brian Pieters/Masterfile; © Spencer Grant/PhotoEdit

81 © Gianni Dagli Orti/CORBIS

82 (top to bottom) © David Young-Wolff/PhotoEdit; © Barbara Penoyar/PhotoDisc/Getty Images

83 (top to bottom) © David Young-Wolff/PhotoEdit; © Barbara Penoyar/PhotoDisc/Getty Images